THE SPIRIT-CONTROLLED WOMAN

Beverly LaHaye

THE SPIRIT-CONTROLLED WOMAN

Beverly LaHaye

HARVEST HOUSE PUBLISHERS
EUGENE, OREGON 97402

Spirit-Controlled Woman

© 1976
Harvest House Publishers
Eugene, Oregon 97402

Library of Congress Catalog Card Number 76-5562
ISBN 0-89081-020-6

Printed in the United States of America

This book is dedicated to the three who gave me the greatest encouragement to put in writing some of the concepts and experiences God has shared with me: first of all to my husband, Tim, for his love, understanding and prayers, and then to Bob Hawkins and Joyce Landorf who gave me the extra push I needed to finally get started.

FOREWORD

Dearest Bev,

For years I have been asked to write a book on temperament and the Spirit-filled life from the woman's point of view. I have recognized the need for such a work, but my problem is, I don't think like a woman. That job needed to be done by a member of the "fairer sex." Obviously that leaves me out.

When Bob Hawkins urged you to write such a book, I heartily agreed for two reasons. For years you have been immersed in the concept of the four temperaments and I can testify that since you surrendered yourself completely to God some thirteen years ago, your temperament has been controlled by the Holy Spirit. I have witnessed a sweet, soft-spirited worry machine that was afraid of your own shadow become transformed into a gracious, outgoing, radiant woman that God has used to inspire thousands of women to accept Him and the abundant life He offers through your lectures on the Spirit-filled life.

It has been fun watching you burn the midnight oil writing this book. Thirteen years ago you would have been frightened off the first page. Now you have trusted Him who is able to do exceedingly abundantly above all that we can ask or think—and it is finished.

I think you've done a great job and will join you in prayer that the concepts you have shared so effectively through your public ministry will now bless thousands more through the reading of this book. I will also pray that many of them will enjoy the same transformation you have.

To be very honest, I prefer the new Beverly. Oh, I've always loved you; after all, I'm commanded to! But since you became a Spirit-filled woman, I find you much more exciting and easier to love. I have a hunch other husbands will have the same experience after their wives learn the joys of being a *Spirit-Controlled Woman*. I sure thank God for sending you into my life!

With All My Love,
Tim

TABLE OF CONTENTS

1

THE MISSING DIMENSION

Thirteen years ago I discovered what was really missing in my life. Before that time I had been a fearful, introverted person with a rather poor self-image. As a young wife I was constantly fearful of not living up to the expectations of our friends. It was difficult for me to entertain in our home because of this. I refused most invitations to speak to women's groups because I felt very inadequate and questioned if I really had anything to say to them. After all, who wants to hear what a young woman has to say whose only accomplishment in life was giving birth to four children? One very well-meaning lady said to me in the early days of our ministry, "Mrs. LaHaye, our last pastor's wife was an author; what do you do?'' That was a heavy question for a fearful 27-year-old woman to cope with. And I began to wonder, ''What did I do?'' Oh yes, I was a good mother to my four children, I could keep house reasonably well, my husband adored me, but what could I do that would be eternally effective in the lives of other women? The answer seemed to come back to me, ''Very little!'' There was something missing in my life—something that could give me the confidence and the self-assuredness that ''I can do all things through Christ who strengtheneth me'' (Phil. 4:13).

When I was at a conference at Forest Home, California, I heard for the first time about the filling of the Holy Spirit and the effect it could have on my future. This was the missing dimension in my life. The fear that possessed me was not of God, ''For God hath not given us the spirit of fear; but of power, and of love, and of a sound mind'' (2 Tim. 1:7). This is what I needed! I needed power, love, and a sound mind to step forth in all confidence and let God do whatever He chose to do with my life. I could only do this through the filling of the Holy Spirit. I came to realize that I was wrong in not accepting myself just as God had created me—I was a special creation from His own hand! (Psa. 139:14). So at this conference I simply asked God to fill me with the Holy Spirit and to do the impossible thing through me by this new power within. There was no outward sign or expression except for a beautiful, quiet peace that settled in my heart and the new confidence that God was going to do something far better with my life than I had been able to do. It was an experience that only God and I knew about. I had a new power within me to do the impossible for God. The missing dimension had been found!

I have watched God perform miracle after miracle over the last thirteen years. As I look back over those years and see the marvelous changes that have taken place, I realize it has only been possible as a result of the Holy Spirit having taken complete control of every part of my life.

2

THE FOUR
BASIC TEMPERAMENTS
OF WOMEN

The study of the four temperaments has greatly influenced my life over the past twelve years. My husband has used it in seminar after seminar, and I have seen the great effect it has had in the lives of individuals when they began to understand why they behave the way they do and that there is help for their weaknesses. Temperament may explain our behavior, but it will not excuse it. Temperament, as a part of our human nature, must be controlled by our spiritual nature. It is true that our basic temperaments do not change. However, the weaknesses of these temperaments can be trained, disciplined, and even corrected by the help of the Holy Spirit. We must determine what features in our temperaments interfere with our spiritual growth and then begin a spiritual renovating to overcome these weaknesses. The idea of recognizing the strengths and weaknesses of each temperament helps us to understand ourselves and each other so much better. When we know that through the Holy Spirit our weaknesses can be modified, we can begin to take on the traits of the Spirit-controlled temperament. This has changed my husband and me as individuals and our relationship to each other.

Several times women have asked when something would be written from the woman's point of view regarding the four temperaments. So, using two of my husband's books, *Spirit-Controlled Temperament* and *Transformed Temperaments,* plus *Temperament and the Christian Faith* by O. Hallesby as the basis for my resource material, I would like to share these concepts that God has given me for women.

Please realize that this is not intended to be a complete study of the four temperaments; for that information you may read the three books mentioned above. The purpose of this book is an attempt to relate practical everyday situations to the temperaments, showing how you would expect each one to act or react and how the Holy Spirit can affect every area of a woman's life.

We are admonished in Gal. 5:16 to "walk in the Spirit and ye shall not fulfill the lusts of the flesh." It is not too difficult to put on a "Spirit-controlled" front on Sundays or when things are going to please us. The true test of walking in the Spirit will not be the way we *act* but the way we *react* to the daily frustrations of life.

Before we see what changes the Holy Spirit can make

in the life of each individual woman, it would be wise to look at the basic temperaments with their strengths and weaknesses. Keep in mind that no one is made up of one temperament only; every individual is composed of a varying combination of the four temperaments. Some will be blended with two, three, or possibly even all four. The important factor is to determine your predominant temperament and then to consider your strengths and weaknesses as well as the way the Holy Spirit can increase your strengths and help you overcome your weaknesses.

We will consider the four temperaments in the following order:

   I. Melancholic
  II. Phlegmatic
 III. Choleric
 IV. Sanguine

I. Martha Melancholy

Martha Melancholy is the introvert, and we sometimes think of her as having the "suffering" temperament because she is so hard on herself through constant self-examination. She is naturally a dark, gloomy, and pessimistic person, yet she is a very gifted, genius-prone individual.

Occupation and Hobbies

  ✓Artist
  ✓Musician
   Seamstress
   Culinary Arts
   Accountant

Beautician
Spectator at athletic events
Educator—usually in math, science, or English
Interior Decorator
Fashion Designer
Author
Crafts
Poet—either to write or to enjoy

Emotions

Strengths
Loves music and art
Rich, sensitive nature
Analytical ability
Emotionally responsive
Deep, reflective thinker
Weaknesses
Moody and gloomy
Pessimistic; always looking on the negative
Likes to suffer; martyr
Hypochrondriac
Introspective to the point of being harmful
Depression
Proud

Relationship to others

Strengths
Dependable friend
Self-sacrificing friend
Faithful and loyal friend
Makes friends cautiously
Deep feeling for friends

Weaknesses

Critical of others' imperfections

Searches for perfection and judges everything according to her ideals

Fearful of what others think of her

Suspicious of others

Can erupt into violent anger after prolonged animosity

Often deeply hurt by others

Will carry a grudge and be revengeful

Dislikes those in opposition

Hard to get along with

Activities

Strengths

Strong perfectionist tendencies

Likes detail and analytical work

Self-disciplined; finishes what she undertakes

Fitted for creative, intellectual work

Conscientious and thorough

Gifted; genius-prone

Knows her own limitations

Weaknesses

Indecisive

Theoretical and impractical

Tires easily

Hesitant to start a new project

Too much analysis; leads to discouragement

Life work must demand the greatest in sacrifice, self-denial and service

Gets moody over creations

II. Polly Phlegmatic

Polly Phlegmatic is a super-introvert and has a

unique calmness about her which gives her a slow, easy-going, and "well-balanced" temperament. She is stubborn and indecisive and resigned to the fate before her.

Occupations and Hobbies

Homemaker
Good mother
Bookkeeper
Counselor
Teacher—elementary
Crafts
✓Reluctant leader
Administrator
Seamstress
Secretary
Gourmet cook
✓Spectator of athletics

Emotions

Strengths
Calm and dependable
✓Good-natured and easy to get along with
Cheerful and pleasant even if she doesn't have much to say
Kind-hearted
Peace-loving
Weaknesses
Lacks confidence in self
Pessimistic and fearful; worrier
Rarely laughs aloud
Passive and indifferent

Compromising

Self-righteous

Relationship to others

Strengths

Pleasant to be with

Has many friends

Dry, witty sense of humor

Softening and conciliating effect upon others

Constant and faithful

Diplomatic and peacemaker

Good listener

Faithful friend

Gives advice only when asked

Weaknesses

Doesn't allow herself to get involved

Selfish and stingy

Studies people with indifference

Unenthusiastic

Stubborn

Indifferent about others

Teases others who annoy her

Not too cordial

Attitude of superiority

Activities

Strengths

Works well under pressure

Practical, easy way of working

Conservative

Neat and proficient

Plans her work before beginning

Stabilizing influence

Dependable worker

Weaknesses

Calm, serene, uninvolved spectator in life

Slow and lazy

Reluctant leader

Lack of motivation

Indecisive

Overprotects herself from involvement

Discourages others

Opposes change of any kind

III. Clara Choleric

Clara Choleric is an extrovert and probably the greatest producer of all; this gives her the right to be called the "active" temperament. She is very self-confident and has a strong will.

Occupations and Hobbies

Strong leader

Professional career

President of women's work

> Home entertainer
> Executive secretary
> Participant in athletics
> President of local P.T.A.
> Administrator
> High school teacher
> Precinct worker
> Bank trust officer
> Crusader

Emotions

Strengths
> Confident and strong to make decisions
> Strong-willed and self-determined
> ✓Optimistic
> ✓Self-sufficient
> Fearless and bold

Weaknesses
> Violent anger problem
> Highly opinionated
> Insensitive to needs of others
> Unemotional and cold
> Little appreciation for aesthetics
> Unsympathetic and harsh
> Impetuous and violent
> Disgusted by tears

Relationship to others

Strengths
> Does not expect anyone else to do something she can't do
> Not easily discouraged
> Strong leader

✓Good judge of people
 Motivator of others
 Exhorter
✓Never daunted by circumstances
Weaknesses
    Lack of compassion
    Makes decisions for others
    Cruel, blunt, and sarcastic
    Tends to dominate a group
    Arrogant and bossy
    Uses people for own benefit
    Unforgiving and revengeful
✓Prone to bigotry
    Haughty and domineering

Activities

    Strengths
        Good organizer and promoter
        Decisive; intuitive ability to make decisions
        Quick and bold in emergencies
        Keen, quick mind
        Great capacity for action
        Does not vacillate
        Very practical
        Stimulates others to activity
        Thrives on opposition
        Sets goals and reaches them.
    Weaknesses
        Overly self-confident
        Crafty
✓Prejudiced
        Opinionated

Bored by details
Non-analytical
Forces others to agree to her plan of work
Tiresome and hard to please
Only time for her own plans or projects

IV. Sarah Sanguine

Sarah Sanguine is the super-extrovert, and with her outgoing spirit and her charisma she can rightly be called the "enjoyable" temperament. She is warm and lively and certainly the life of the party.

Occupations and Hobbies

Actress
Woman's speaker
Saleswoman
Visiting and caring for sick
Good cook
Volunteer work
Loving mother
Foster home parent
Leader
Given to hospitality
Receptionist
Participant in athletics

Emotions

Strengths
Warm and lively
Charisma
Talkative—never at a loss for words
Carefree—never worries about the future or frets about the past

Great storyteller

Lives in present

Conversation has an infectious quality

Unusual capacity for enjoyment

Weaknesses

Cries easily

Emotionally unpredictable

Restless

Spontaneous anger

Exaggerates the truth

Appears phony

Lacks self-control

Emotional decisions; impulsive buyer

Naive and childlike

Comes on too strong

Relationship to others

Strengths

Makes friends easily

Responsive to people

Enjoyable and optimistic

Always friendly and smiling to others

Easy to apologize

Tender and sympathetic

Converses with genuine warmth

Shares other people's joys and sorrows

Weaknesses

Dominates conversation

Not attentive

Weak-willed and little conviction

Seeks credit and approval

Enjoys people and then forgets them

Makes excuses for negligence
Talks too often about herself
Forgets promises and obligations

Activities

Strengths
Makes good first impression
Not bored because she lives in the present
Gifted in caring for the sick
Easily engages in new plans or projects
Breeds enthusiasm
Weaknesses
Completely disorganized
Undependable; late
Undisciplined
Wastes time talking when should be working
Many unfinished projects
Easily distracted
Falls short of goal

3

YOU CAN HELP YOURSELF!

Be yourself! Your temperament is a permanent part of you which will stay with you from start to finish. It will change somewhat during certain periods of your life as you mature through childhood, teen years, and adulthood. Enjoy the richness of those strengths in your temperament; then ask God for help to modify the weaknesses that you might become more Spirit-filled and Christ-like. Those weaknesses that hinder your relationship with Jesus Christ are a sin. Whenever you indulge in one of the weaknesses of your temperament, you can be sure that you will grieve or quench the Holy Spirit. That is sin!

And grieve not the Holy Spirit of God, whereby ye are sealed unto the day of redemption. Let all bitterness, and wrath, and anger, and clamour, and evil speaking, be put away from you, with all malice: And be ye kind one to another, tenderhearted, forgiving one another, even as God for Christ's sake hath forgiven you.

Eph. 4:30-32

See that none render evil for evil unto any man; but ever follow that which is good, both among yourselves, and to all men. Rejoice evermore. Pray without ceasing. In everything give thanks: for this is the will of God in Christ Jesus concerning you. Quench not the Spirit.

1 Thess. 5:15-19

If you are a Christian, then you already have access to the power of the Holy Spirit to help you overcome your weaknesses. As long as you have sin in your heart, you cannot expect the Holy Spirit to give you victory over these shortcomings.

If I regard iniquity in my heart, the Lord will not hear me.
Psalms 66:18

The first thing you need to do is to follow the instructions given in 1 John 1:9:

If we confess our sins, he is faithful and just to forgive us our sins, and to cleanse us from all unrighteousness.

Every time you grieve or quench the Holy Spirit, it is necessary to confess your sin and then thank God for His forgiveness and restoration. Follow the advice in Eph. 5:18 to be filled with the Spirit.

And be not drunk with wine, wherein is excess; but be filled with the Spirit.

This means to be dominated or controlled by the Holy Spirit.

One of the most confusing aspects of the filling of the

Holy Spirit is our inability to understand the true meaning of the word "filled." We tend to think of filling a glass or container, but that is not what the Scripture means when it compares a Spirit-filled Christian to a wine-filled drunk. The drunk is not literally filled with wine; he is *controlled* by it. His staggering, reeling movements are uncoordinated because he is controlled by alcohol. In like manner the Spirit-filled Christian woman is going to be controlled by the Holy Spirit. That is, instead of performing the weaknesses of her temperament, she will manifest the fruits of the Spirit—love, joy, peace, longsuffering, gentleness, goodness, faith, meekness, temperance. You must be willing to let go of yourself and be controlled by God to do anything with your life the Holy Spirit desires to do. Ask for this kind of filling and thank God for what He is going to do in your life, believing that He will do it.

> In everything give thanks; for this is the will of God in Christ Jesus concerning you.
>
> *1 Thess. 5:18*
>
> Now thanks be unto God, which always causeth us to triumph in Christ, and maketh manifest the savour of his knowledge by us in every place.
>
> *2 Cor. 2:14*

Here are some suggestions how the weaknesses of each temperament can be modified when controlled by the Holy Spirit:

Martha Melancholy

Emotions—Her deep, dark moods of gloom and depression will take on a more happy, cheerful spirit. The introspective nature can learn to step out on faith and look toward the future with bright optimism.

Relationship to Others—The Holy Spirit will help her to develop a loving spirit, thus causing her to be less critical and suspicious of others and much easier to get along with.

Activities—She will become more outgoing and less self-centered. Her pessimism will be counteracted by a thanksgiving spirit if she is obedient to the Lord and keeps her eyes on Him and not on herself.

Greatest Needs—

To overcome her critical spirit.

To be delivered from self-absorption.

To become occupied in loving service for others, thus forgetting herself.

To develop a thanksgiving spirit.

Summary—The self-sacrificing, thinking Martha Melancholy is probably the most gifted of all the temperaments. And yet, because of her self-centeredness, her critical spirit and her gloom, she suffers more than any of the others and limits her ability to use her talents and gifts. It is only when her heart and mind are controlled by the Holy Spirit that she can forget herself and her critical spirit and become a genuine Christian who helps those around her with a tender and sensitive nature. She can develop a thanksgiving heart that will become a pattern of living for her. Only then can she find fulfillment, peace, and satisfaction in Christ.

Some time ago I counseled a Martha Melancholy type who was very concerned about the future. Her husband was not the man she thought she had married. He was not sufficiently productive, not ambitious, very untidy, not helpful around the house, not even sexy enough, and she felt that life had not dealt fairly with her. She was experiencing deep moods of depression and had even contemplated ending her life.

After listening to her steady stream of problems, I pointed out that all her statements had been critical of her husband and the way he had been unfair by not meeting up to the standards she had placed on him. I thought perhaps this fellow was a complete dud, but my last try was to send her back home for a week to develop a list of only the positive, good things she could find in his character. I told her that if she was having difficulty finding anything to put on her list, she might have to ask God for help. She came back the following week and said for the first three days she had nothing to report. Finally, she asked God to help her to see if there was any good in this man. Her list then consisted of four things: (1) he was good to the children, (2) he was generous with his money, (3) he was respected at their church as a fine Bible teacher, and (4) he was faithful to her. Her critical spirit of this man was ruining their marriage and her life. She confessed this as sin and asked God to help her to stop being so critical and judging him by her own ideals and standards. One year passed and I heard from her again. She just wanted me to know how thankful she was for her husband! He still had some of the same faults but she had discovered that he also had some very great strengths and she thanked God for this man.

Martha Melancholy has such great potential! Because she is naturally a loyal friend, when Jesus Christ becomes her Lord and Saviour and she is controlled by the Holy Spirit, there is no other temperament that has a greater dedication and devotion to God.

Polly Phlegmatic

Emotions—Her fearful, worrying nature will be replaced with the self-confidence of the Spirit-filled life. Her pessimism will gradually turn to optimism.

Relationship to Others—She will develop a new love for people and will desire to get involved with others, thus taking away the selfishness and the indifference that she formerly knew.

Activities—The Holy Spirit will help her to lose her slowness and laziness. She will develop new motivation for productivity as she becomes involved and senses the needs of those about her.

Greatest Needs—

To overcome her passivity.

To learn to give of herself to others.

To stop acting like a Christian and really be one.

To recognize her fearfulness as a sin and cope with it accordingly.

Summary—The complacent, peaceful Polly Phlegmatic is probably the easiest to be around because of her easy-going and well-balanced nature. She usually holds everyone off at arm's length and protects herself from getting too involved with people or work. Her greatest need is to recognize that her fear, which is not of God, definitely limits her effectiveness for Christ. She needs to face her indolence as a sin; then she should become involved with Jesus Christ and in giving of herself to others. She is a capable person when she is willing to let go of herself and let God take control.

There are many Polly Phlegmatics in our group of friends across the country, but very few of them will ever seek help even when they recognize they have a problem. There is one Polly in particular that comes to my mind. She was just about as fearful and introverted as I have ever know. On the surface her friends were never aware that she had this turmoil going on inside. She presented herself to others as a very calm, self-confident, and capable person. But one day she seemed to come unglued and confessed to me that what she represented on the outside was not at all what was taking place on the inside. Even phlegmatics have their breaking point. She confessed how fearful she was of other people and how inadequate she thought she was. When asked to serve on a board in the church, she refused with a flimsy excuse. This had been repeated many times over in various positions of leadership and ministry. It was then that she began to realize that she was cheating herself from many opportunities to serve Christ by her fear and indifference. Her children and her husband were all active in the ministry of their church. She was the one on the outside—uninvolved, indifferent, and super-negative. This was beginning to show in her mental attitude toward her family and the church. On one particular day, this dear lady was faced with the reality that she was being left "in the dust" spiritually. Her husband and children were outgrowing her as a result of her fear and selfishness. I read 2 Tim. 1:7 from my Bible, "For God hath not given us the spirit of fear; but of power, and of love, and of a sound mind." She genuinely confessed her sin to Christ and prayed to be filled with the Holy Spirit, asking God to do a beautiful thing in her life. She desired not just to be involved in the ministry of her church but also to be a warm, loving, motivated, godly woman freed from the fears that bound her within.

I have watched this Polly turn from a woman paralyzed by her own fears to a beautiful example of the Spirit-filled woman. Her husband and children are pleased and proud of the new lady at their house. It has been like watching a rose bud open into its full maturity as a beautiful sweet-smelling flower, bringing joy and leaving a fragrance with all those who come in contact with her.

Clara Choleric

Emotions—Her worst enemy is her violent anger problem. She can expect the Holy Spirit to help her get this under control as she commits it to God.

Relationship to Others—The Holy Spirit will give her a compassionate heart and help her to become more forgiving and thoughtful, less sarcastic and bossy, and willing to listen to the concerns of other people.

Activities—She will seek to be open-minded and less opinionated. The realization will come to her that other people tend to have some very good ideas also, and she can put her efforts behind accomplishing their projects.

Greatest Needs—

To become sensitive to the needs of others.

To confess her angry and cruel spirit.

To develop her inner beauty by quiet hours spent reading the Bible and praying.

Summary—The lively, energetic Clara Choleric can outproduce all the other temperaments put together. However, to reach her goals she probably has offended and run roughshod over the feelings of the other milder temperaments that may have stood in her way. When she allows the Holy Spirit to soften her insensitivity to others and learns to love with a compassionate heart, she can be a mighty crusader for the cause of Jesus Christ.

A very upset Clara Choleric stood before me one night pouring out her broken heart. When a choleric gets to this place, she has had to go through a very traumatic experience which she could not control or manipulate. She was frustrated, angry and broken and had finally come to me for help.

I had just finished speaking that evening at the first session of a weekend women's retreat. The four basic temperaments had been presented with their strengths and weaknesses. As I unfolded the story of cholerics, I pointed out that they were untiring drivers, who usually dominated and made decisions for everyone around them. In addition, they were often hostile and cruel women. The Holy Spirit seemed to use this description of the choleric to reach Clara's heart. She was all of these and more. Through her hot tears she told me the story of her fifteen-year-old son who had finally had all of this angry woman he could take and had run away from home. She had bossed her husband around and tried to dominate him until she had driven him to alcohol. The pastor of her church had tried to help her earlier in her life, but she became angry at him and refused his help. Clara had blown up and told off the congregation and was now left with not too many friends. In fact, she said that her relatives did not like to spend holidays with her be-cause she usually had an explosion of anger before the day was over. This dear lady had finally come to the end of her rope and was able to hear the Holy Spirit speaking to her about her miserable condition.

Together we prayed as she asked forgiveness for her sinful wretchedness and then asked to be filled or controlled by the Holy Spirit. She prayed especially that she might learn to give love, to like people, and to control her violent temper. I wish I could report that after praying this prayer for forgiveness her husband immediately stopped his drinking and her son came home. But I am sorry to say that Clara must bear the scars she has made on other members of her family. She can only trust God to change her so completely that her family will see the transformation in her life and be willing to change. If only Clara had made this decision earlier in her life, if only she had allowed her minister to help her many years ago, she could have been saved from the heartaches caused by her anger.

Sarah Sanguine

Emotions—The sanguine lady is a very emotional gal. She is never very far from tears and usually unstable. The Holy Spirit can stabilize her emotions and calm her restless spirit. She can develop self-control and a disciplined life with God's help.

Relationship to Others—She will become a genuine friend and show more interest and concern with the lives of other people than the other temperaments. Her attention on herself will have to be minimized to be a Spirit-filled sanguine.

Activities—Unfinished projects and disorganization should become a thing of the past as she matures in her Christian life. With the help of the Holy Spirit she will certainly be a more productive person.

Greatest Needs—

To be more reliable and dependable.

To develop a greater self-disciplined life.

To replace her ego with genuine humility.

Summary—The warm-hearted, loquacious Sarah Sanguine is the most outgoing of all the temperaments. She has the unique ability to enjoy each moment as it comes. This causes her many problems, however, because while enjoying this moment, she has completely forgotten what she promised in the previous moments. The Holy Spirit will help her to be more dependable and faithful when she recognizes her need and asks God for help in this area. She has the potential of being a delightful and productive Christian when she becomes self-disciplined and lets the Holy Spirit control her life.

Sarah is by far the most fun-loving and outgoing temperament of all. However, she suffers a great deal because of her noisy mannerisms, self-indulgence, and weak will. I saw this vividly portrayed in the life of a typical Sarah Sanguine. This gal was a very friendly, outgoing person but her loud laughter and noisy remarks caused many of her friends to keep their distance. She usually entered a room with her mouth first. Her melancholic husband was extremely aggravated by her excessive talking and high-pitched laughter. He constantly tried to get her to be a quieter person like himself. This caused much frustration for her because she was not a naturally quiet person. She began to take her frustrations out by eating between-meal and bedtime snacks, which resulted in a rapid increase in her weight. And because she suffered from a weak will and self-indulgence problem, the snacking and stuffing became uncontrollable. I watched Sarah put on twenty to thirty pounds in a short time. This additional problem caused her melancholic husband to be disgusted with her lack of self-control. Little did he realize that he had been the initial cause of the situation. Finally, in desperation she came to me asking what she should do. I first suggested that she and her husband read *Spirit-Controlled Temperament* and learn the strengths and weaknesses of each of their temperaments. I felt it was necessary for the husband to understand that a sanguine could never be as quiet as a melancholic. Then Sarah had to face her own individual problem and realize that her lack of self-control could be improved by the filling of the Holy Spirit. She needed to learn temperance, gentleness, peace, and faith. Her prayer was a very simple genuine petition asking for divine help, not only with her weight problem but also with her blustering laughter. She asked to be filled with the Holy Spirit and to experience the fruit of the Spirit as a result.

Her problems did not change overnight. It was necessary for her to daily commit herself to God for help in these areas. During this time her husband, too, was gaining a new understanding and admiration for the strengths the sanguine lady has to offer. He began to realize what joy and cheer his sanguine wife had brought into his dark, dreary life.

Sarah has gradually trimmed off the extra pounds she had gained, and her noisy, blustering sounds seemed to have changed to cheerful, happy, contented laughter that is both pleasing and contagious. The two of them are a beautiful example of how opposites can complement one another when controlled by the Holy Spirit. Without the Holy Spirit, opposites can produce great friction that causes sparks throughout their lifetime.

4

SINGLE—
CHOICE OR CHANCE

We women are fortunate—God is not a respecter of age, sex, or position. He is able to be all-sufficient for single as well as married women. All members of the female sex spend part of their lives as singles, some more than others. But the same instruction is given to all, regardless of their marital status—"Let us also walk in the Spirit" (Eph. 5:25).

The time-honored idea that one must be an older married woman in order to be a Spirit-filled Christian is not necessarily true.

Tender Teen-ager

Several years ago when our children were very young,

we had a teen-age girl come to babysit for our family one evening. When we returned home that night, there was time for a short visit with her. We asked about school, her family, etc. and then talked to her about her relationship with Christ. She quickly responded, "I'm a Christian but I don't want to get too spiritual and that stuff until I get older. I want to enjoy myself while I'm young." Many years later this same girl told us how sorry she was that she had wasted so many years of her life and how she had come very close to ruining it.

Teen-age girls can be Spirit-filled and not be square! I have seen many examples of this in our own church. What can be more beautiful than to see a lovely, vivacious teen-age girl completely sold on Jesus Christ. One girl in particular comes to my mind. She is not beautiful, nor is she ugly; she is rather plain and average. This gal is a steady witness for Christ and liked by all her peers, especially the males. She has problems that would cause some teen-agers to buckle under, but not her. Instead, she has committed every area of her life, problems and all, to Jesus Christ. Is she square? Not on your life! She is totally committed to Christ and truly a Spirit-controlled teen-age gal.

I have seen two areas of her life change completely during her teen years. One is her relationship with her parents. A rebellious girl cannot be a Spirit-filled Christian. The Bible clearly states, "Children, obey your parents" and "Honor thy father and mother." When she desired to please God in all things, it was necessary for her to commit her rebellion and to obey God's plan for respecting her parents. She now has a very happy Mom and Dad, and together they have a beautiful relationship!

The other area that has drastically changed is her self-acceptance. When she realized that God had accepted her as she was, problems and all, she began to change her ideas. She had been measuring herself by the world's yardstick. Her vision was blurred by the bitterness and resentment she felt towards her Creator. When other things in her life were confessed and corrected, she began to accept the fact that she was a custom-made individual, prepared for a specific purpose by the hand of God.

Dare to Date

Girls, you need to have clearly established convictions before you dare to date. The ground rules should be made in your own mind before you ever leave home. It is too late to try to decide what rules to play by when in the middle of a clinch in a parked car. God has definite ideas on dating. Remember that you are a child for whom He gave His only Son. Does He care who you date, where you go, and how you conduct yourself? He surely does! If your desire is to have a Spirit-controlled date life, then you must consider what God desires for you. 2 Corinthians 6:14 tells very clearly the kind of man God wants you to marry:

> Be ye not unequally yoked together with unbelievers; for what fellowship hath righteousness with unrighteousness? And what communion hath light with darkness?

Of course, we are talking about dating not marriage, but the two are definitely related: one sure way to prevent marrying a non-Christian is never date a non-Christian.

When God said, "Children, obey your parents," He certainly had in mind teen-age girls. If your Mom and Dad have rules and standards for your dating, thank God for parents who love you and want to guard against the temptations that surround you during this period in your life. When a fellow helps you obey your dating rules, it shows real strength of character on his part.

One of our daughters came to a crossroad in her dating life when she had to make a decision between obeying her parents and pleasing her date. This boy seemed to bristle under the dating rules we set for our daughter. Time and time again he would call on the phone and try to rearrange things and get us to bend our rules this way or that. It put our daughter under a great deal of pressure, and tension seemed to mount between us every time he would call. Finally, our daughter decided she had had enough and told him that he had to make a choice—either to date her with her parents' rules just as they were or not to date her at all. The young man decided after several days not to date her anymore. He boldly stated that she was used to more discipline than he and that he just didn't want to be that disciplined. This was not a happy time for our daughter, but spiritually she grew two feet that day. To us it proved that the young man was not really meant for our daughter anyway. We wanted her to marry a man with the strength of character and discipline necessary to do the thing that was right even when it wasn't his choice. We have learned that young people who rebel against their parents' rules are prone to rebel against God and eventually each other.

Before You Say "I Do"

> Wherefore be ye not unwise but understanding what the will of the Lord is.

Ephesians 5:17

When you fall in love, it becomes difficult to always

think straight and to be objective regarding the Lord's will for your life. The time to start seeking God's leading is before love begins; once you're in love, your heart can play tricks on you. Since you will probably fall in love only with someone you have dated, ask God at the very start who you should date. Following this plan will keep you on the right path and will help you to be sane and sober in choosing your partner for life. What kind of a man should you consider marrying? Just looking for a tall, dark, and handsome man is not good enough. Those features will be short-lived, since all tall, dark, and handsome men are not necessarily good marriage partners. This "dream man" will be one you must sit across the table from day after day. He will be there to see you at your best moments and at your worst. There will be days when he will not be the man of your dreams—unless they are nightmares. But you will marry him "for better or for worse, for richer or for poorer, in sickness and in health, till death do us part." At a time like this his height, shade of complexion, or good looks will have nothing to do with how he wears as a good husband day after day and year after year. What is this man really like? Look beyond his outward appearance and consider what the real "man of the heart" is like.

   . . . Is he a man of good character and integrity?
   . . . What is his relationship to Jesus Christ?
   . . . Is he active in the work of a good Bible-believing church?
   . . . Is he kind and thoughtful to others?
   . . . How does he treat his mother?
   . . . Does he talk only about himself?
   . . . How much interest does he show in your needs

and concerns?

. . . Is he able to control his physical attraction to you?

. . . Does he consider your reputation and value your moral convictions and standards?

. . . Does he treat you like a lady?

. . . Is he ready to love you as Christ loves the Church?

Husbands, love your wives even as Christ also loved the church and gave himself for it that he might sanctify and cleanse it with the washing of water by the word, that he might present it to himself a glorious church, not having spot or wrinkle or any such thing, but that it should be holy and without blemish. So ought men to love their wives as their own bodies. He that loveth his wife loveth himself. For no man ever yet hated his own flesh, but nourisheth and cherisheth it, even as the Lord the church. For we are members of his body, of his flesh, and of his bones. For this cause shall a man leave his father and mother and shall be joined unto his wife, and they two shall be one flesh. This is a great mystery, but I speak concerning Christ and the church. Nevertheless, let every one of you in particular so love his wife even as himself; and the wife, see that she reverence her husband.

Eph. 5:25-33

Girls, look him over carefully. Ask all the questions you care to. It is far better to ask now than to wish you had in years to come.

Of all the temperaments, Martha Melancholy is more likely to ask questions and ask questions and ask questions. She is looking for the perfect man! She may fall in love with who she thinks is the "ideal man," only to find that he is human and has some weaknesses. She will then be inclined to break the engagement and call off the wedding. This is far better than leaving him after the wedding is over; however, she needs to understand that the Holy Spirit is able to help the two of them overcome their weaknesses. She has them, too! How beautiful it is when a young couple can prayerfully enter the wedding relationship together, asking for the filling of the Spirit to blend their strengths and weaknesses and unite them as one.

Martha may be mistaken as an unfriendly snob when really she is not. Because she is withdrawn and tends to be a loner, she gives the impression of being unfriendly. Boys feel uncomfortable around her and may not be too eager to ask her for a date. Her personality and social life would be greatly improved if she could trust God to help her develop a friendly, more outgoing spirit.

Polly Phlegmatic is likely to have several boyfriends because she is so easygoing and pleasant to be with. However, Polly is very timid and lacks confidence. Of all the temperaments, she will probably be the most surprised when her future husband proposes and will wonder why he ever wanted her.

In a recent survey that my husband and I took in preparation for our new book, *The Act of Marriage,* we discovered that the phlegmatic woman engaged in premarital sex far more than the phlegmatic man. Because she is usually involved with a man of a stronger temperament and is usually eager to please, she is more likely to give in even against her convictions. It is at this point that she desperately needs the discerning wisdom of the Holy Spirit to sort out what God's plan is for her life. There is no need for her to be swept along with the emotions of her lover. God can stabilize her and help her to evaluate the total picture before she makes the final commitment to her prospective husband.

Clara Choleric may likely be the girl who wants to get married quickly and get on with the program. She is inclined to rush into marriage without analyzing the pros and cons or evaluating her relationship and future with this man. She is probably confident that whatever problems face her in the future, she will be able to tackle them head-on. Her greatest need at this time is to slow down and wait for the leading of the Holy Spirit in her life. God has a plan for her and she must move according to His time schedule.

Sarah Sanguine is such a lover by nature that she will probably fall in and out of love several times before she settles down. She is so friendly and outgoing that many boys mistake her for a flirt and are swept off their feet. A girl has to learn the difference between being a flirt and being a snob. Somewhere there is a happy medium that makes a woman truly free instead of inhibited, self-conscious, or overly aggressive. God's love in her life will be reflected in her genuine, warm friendliness and her gracious spirit and will give her the proper balance in her friendships. Because Sarah is naive and often child-like, she needs a special hedge of protection built around her by the Holy Spirit. She is easily talked into anything and could make a wrong decision that would affect her entire life. Her sympathetic and compassionate heart could lead her to marry because of sympathy and not love. Sarah needs to be a Spirit-filled dating girl, as all temperaments do, but she especially needs divine help in developing strong convictions and the strength of character to live by them.

Thoughtless Temptation

The next subject may be a sore spot; nevertheless, I feel compelled to proceed. What about "turning on" a guy? Sad to say, many Christian girls and women are rather thoughtless about this. I have seen lovely girls conduct themselves in such a manner that they turn fellows on and cause them to have problems with lust and evil thoughts. One charming young lady was walking out of church with her hand in her date's arm and was very carelessly allowing her breast to rub against the boy. Is it possible that she was not even aware of what she was doing to him? On another occasion I saw a darling girl snuggled next to her date in church; during the sermon she reached over and placed her hand on his leg. It looked very innocent, but I could almost hear the fireworks going off in the pew across the aisle.

One thing that every girl should keep in mind is that her body is the temple of the Holy Spirit. 2 Corinthians 6:16 says,

> For ye are the temple of the living God; as God hath said, "I will dwell in them and walk in them, and I will be their God and they shall be my people."

You are not the owner of your own body. You have been bought with a price; therefore, you should glorify God with your body!

This leads to another subject—how do you dress? There are three categories in dress: (1) the suggestive, sexy appeal that seduces, (2) the liberated style which neither seduces nor attracts and is usually not too becoming but which allows the woman to do her own thing and to express her rebellion, or (3) the modest feminine approach that is attractive and becoming to the wearer. The sexy appeal is represented by very short skirts, hot pants, skin-tight clothes, the no-bra look, and plunging necklines which leave little to the male imagination and result in being seductive rather than attractive. The liberated style can be anything from faded jeans to "plain-Jane" or masculine-styled clothing. Such styles may gain frequent stares from passers-by but seldom looks of approval. The feminine appeal is represented by modest clothing that is stylish, attractive, and presents a feminine mystique that ennobles a man. We are to be modest, attractive, appealing, and—most of all—feminine as God made us.

Why do you dress the way you do? Seriously consider this and give yourself an honest answer. Is it because you feel you are only a sex object and that is all you have that can attract the man you want? Your appearance will certainly give that away. Or is it because you are glad to be feminine, proud to be a woman, and you want to represent the kind of person that belongs to God?

In some cases I believe ladies are very innocent of the effect clothes have on a man. I met one such woman recently; she was a fine Christian woman, very active in her church program and probably one of their most faithful week-night evangelistic callers. However, her choice of clothes began to present a problem to some of the men. She wore extremely short dresses that showed off a major portion of her very shapely legs. Finally, the pastor decided to speak to her privately about the stir she was causing and prayed that she would not be offended but would accept what he said in the right spirit. This dear lady had no idea that she was causing a problem or that her clothes were offensive. Her genuine desire was to please the Lord and to be a testimony of Christ living in her. So after thanking the pastor for approaching her in such a gracious manner, she determined to dress in a more modest, Christ-like style. That was the response of a Spirit-filled woman!

Companionship or Confusion

Most single working girls find it necessary to share an apartment with another girl in order to keep living expenses down to a minimum and to supply the need for fellowship that most of us have. This is the true test of your Spirit-filled life and a good preparation for marriage. It is most likely that two opposite temperaments will become roommates and this could be the beginning of their problems. The sanguine girl is more apt to leave her clothes hooked on doorknobs or over the back of chairs, while the choleric is likely to develop a bossy attitude and try to run the household. Both of these could be the source of many heartaches. There will be some girls who have very definite ideas on how the cooking should be done, where the furniture should be arranged, how clean the apartment should be kept, how to spend the grocery budget, and a host of other differences. Be aware of potential problems at the beginning by knowing your roommate—her temperament, her background, her spiritual status. Sometimes bad precedents are set at the start which girls are afraid to break later for fear of hurt feelings.

Many of the people attending the Family Life Seminars where my husband and I speak are single people who are helped tremendously by the temperament study in learning to live with others. This study is also good preparation for marriage. It is a matter of learning to give and take, of not always getting your own way, and of being able to accept the weaknesses and strengths of another person. Ask the Lord to give you wisdom and gentleness and, above all, face each moment under the control of the Spirit.

Beware of an improper physical attachment between you and your roommate. Sad to say, this sometimes happens in today's world, especially if one is lonely, overly affectionate, and lacks a sense of security. This will not happen if you and your roommate are controlled by the Spirit. The secret then is to be sure your relationship with the Lord is right—be sure He is in first place!

Sex and Still Single

Single women have the same basic sex drives that God put into all human beings. Some fortunate girls do not experience this as a problem while others face it as a real struggle in life. So much in our culture today is geared toward participating in a sexual experience. Is it any wonder that sex for singles is more or less taken for granted by the secular community?

Sexual relations with men outside of marriage can be very tempting and readily available for the single woman. A recent article in the August, 1975, issue of *Coronet* magazine gave some rather alarming statistics about sex at the office. A survey of 2500 secretaries revealed that forty percent of them were having lunch hour sex affairs. What motivates secretaries to have sex with their boss if they know there is no chance of marriage? Probably many do so because they are desperately lonely and will pay any price for a period of tenderness even though they know it is only temporary.

An article written by Dr. Robert J. Collins of the Loretto Geriatrics Center of Syracuse, New York *(Journal of the American Medical Association,* April 28, 1975) states that one of the basic flaws in the "new morality" is the assumption that male and female sexuality are the same. With the male, sex can be an activity completely separated from his whole being, while with the female and her complex emotional system, it is her whole existence. Dr. Collins mentions that women claim the tender warm promises and touches are delightful, but the act itself usually leads to an "is that all there is to it?" reaction.

God has very definite ideas about all of this:

> . . . Be not deceived; neither fornicators nor idolaters nor adulterers nor effeminate nor abusers of themselves with mankind nor thieves nor covetous nor drunkards nor revilers nor extortioners shall inherit the kingdom of God. And such were some of you; but ye are washed, but ye are sanctified, but ye are justified in the name of the Lord Jesus and by the Spirit of our God.
>
> *1 Cor. 6:9b-11*

> . . . Now the body is not for fornication, but for the Lord; and the Lord for the body.
>
> *1 Cor. 6:13b*

> Flee fornication. Every sin that a man doeth is outside the body; but he that committeth fornication sinneth against his own body.
>
> *1 Cor. 6:18*

Paul says that some of you were adulterers or fornicators, but now you have been forgiven, sanctified, and justified in the name of the Lord Jesus and by the

Spirit of God. This leaves no exceptions for premarital sex to the woman who desires to be a Spirit-filled person.

Some will think that this is a rather prudish standard because, after all, sex is enjoyable and satisfies a necessary God-given drive. But one aspect that the world rarely talks about when it advocates free-love and promiscuity is the heavy spector of guilt. The Bible teaches that man has a conscience that either accuses him or excuses him, based on his behavior (Romans 2:15). In a practical sense, that accusation renders the ecstasy of the sexual liaison inadequate when compared with the weight of guilt it creates. For the sexual experience only occupies a few moments of time, whereas the burden of guilt must be borne over a lengthy period. Another factor is that it is impossible for any Christian to grow spiritually while violating God's standards of sexual behavior. I have counseled many single ladies who were experiencing depression and spiritual retardation only to find that the real culprit was misuse of their sex drive.

God loves you and is interested in your sexual relations. After all, He created sex. Don't rush ahead of His proper timing for you. One beautiful Christian girl prayed this prayer, "Lord, help me to preserve my body for the one you are preparing for me, and help him to preserve his body for just me!"

Single and Serving

Somewhere along the road a single lady has to face the fact that it is possible God never meant for her to marry and that she may have been selected to live without marrying for the rest of her life. Since there are 109 women to every 100 men, it stands to reason that some will not be able to marry. We ask, "Can God give a woman a full, rich life without marriage?" Is He limited just because she does not have a husband? Of course not. Our relationship to Christ has to be on an individual basis anyway. A husband cannot grow spiritually for his wife. In fact, I can think of some instances where a woman might have been more spiritually advanced had it not been for her husband's interference. Nevertheless, you alone determine your relationship to Christ. Let Christ finish what He has begun in you, "Being confident of this very thing that he who hath begun a good work in you will perform it until the day of Jesus Christ" (Philippians 1:6). The love relationship between you and God is forever, not until you marry or until you die. If He calls you to a single life, He calls you to a special and beautiful relationship with Himself. You can really concentrate on serving the Lord and pleasing only Him.

> The unmarried woman careth for the things of the Lord, that she may be holy both in body and in spirit; but she that is married careth for the things of the world, how she may please her husband. *1 Cor. 7:34*

Your local church offers many areas of Christian service to help you enrich your life. How about teaching a Bible class for other singles, extending Christian hospitality to others in your church, or getting actively involved in your church's calling ministry. A ministry with younger girls—whether it be in Sunday School, Pioneer Girls, etc.—can be a very enriching experience. Our one objective in life, our ultimate desire should be to bring pleasure to the heart of God.

> Thou art worthy, O Lord, to receive glory and honor and power; for thou hast created all things, and for thy plea-

sure they are and were created.

Rev. 4:11

Jesus said,

For whosoever would save his life shall lose it; but whosoever shall lose his life for my sake and the gospel's, the same shall save it.

Mark 8:35

Singlehood is what you make it. It can be a full, rich, and rewarding life or an existence of self-pity and misery. One 26-year-old young lady was so eager to be married that she scared the fellows away. She was obsessed with the idea of getting married so she would not be left to spend her life alone. Another girl, three years her junior and already married, was having severe marital problems. One night in the peak of the turmoil she went to the single girl's apartment to spill out her troubles. After listening to the married woman for two hours she finally realized that she was not so bad off after all. Her apartment became a haven of rest and the walls became a place of tranquility instead of a den of loneliness. She learned to be content where she was.

. . . for I have learned, in whatsoever state I am, therewith to be content.

Phil. 4:11b

5

MARRIED FOR KEEPS

Women have played an important role in the world in spite of what some would have us believe today. Someone has said, "The hand that rocks the cradle rules the world." Another famous statement is, "Behind every successful man is a great woman."

A woman is a necessary part of a man, a part which makes him fulfilled and complete. God created woman very specially from one of Adam's ribs.

> And the Lord God caused a deep sleep to fall upon Adam, and he slept: and he took one of his ribs, and closed up the flesh instead thereof; And the rib, which the Lord God had taken from man, made he a woman, and brought her unto the man.   *Genesis 2:21-22*

Woman is a part of man—not a lesser or greater part, but equal to man. She is God's provision to give man total fulfillment. God designed marriage to be dynamic and fulfilling, and both husband and wife are to be excited about each other. Our married son sent us a beautiful letter about his bride, Kathy, six months after their wedding. He wrote, "Mom and Dad, Kathy is my very best friend." I wish we could say after each beautiful wedding, "And they lived happily ever after, as very best friends." Unfortunately, problems come after two people have lived together for awhile.

Oneness in Christ

The most important goal for every bride and groom is to learn to follow God's principles for marriage. God's designs are true and they work. We cannot function to our maximum as individuals if He is not a major part of our lives. Man and woman are basically self-centered individuals, and marriage is the blending or uniting of two different natures into one. Therefore, it is most important for a happy, successful marriage that both husband and wife are believers in Christ and both have committed their self-centered natures to Him. To reach a oneness in Christ, it is imperative that each partner be filled with the Spirit and have Christ-centered natures.

> If we walk in the light as He Himself is in the light, we have fellowship with one another, and the blood of Jesus, His Son cleanses us from all sin.
>
> *1 John 1:7*

Opposites—Blessing or Curse

Most young lovers see only each other's strengths before marriage. However, most of us are attracted to men who have strengths in the area of our weaknesses. But after marriage the weaknesses of the partners begin to appear.

Marriage tends to pull the weaknesses to the surface. It is then a bride realizes that she did not marry the perfect man as she had thought!

If you had asked me fifteen years ago what weaknesses my husband had that were sources of irritation to me, I could have written a chapter about it. Strange as it may seem, today when I try to think back on those many things that at the time seemed to be driving a deep wedge between us, I find it very difficult to remember. The work of the Holy Spirit in our lives has melted our differences and weaknesses and blended them together to strengthen one another. We need each other. I need my husband's strengths and he needs mine. Together we can be a tower of strength for the work of the Lord because our lives are Spirit-filled.

My husband was asked to perform the wedding ceremony for a lovely young couple. The bride was about as sanguine as one could be while the groom was thoroughly melancholic. The day of the wedding arrived. One hour before the ceremony was to begin, the bride was very joyfully parading up and down the aisles of the church, her gown and veil flowing in the breeze as she passed out the boutonnieres and bouquets. She was smiling radiantly and greeting everyone. This was her wedding day and she was enjoying it to the fullest extent! Meanwhile, my husband was in his study trying to hold up the groom, who was extremely nervous, wondering if anyone was coming to the wedding, if he had the ring, and even if the bride would be there on time. Little did he know what was really going on out in the sanctuary. The ceremony started and everything went along beautifully—until the time came for the couple to kneel at the altar while the soloist sang "The Lord's Prayer." Hearing a little commotion before him, my husband looked down and noticed that copious tears were running down the cheeks of the groom. The bride quickly sized up the situation, looked at my husband with a wink, and reached in her bosom for a handkerchief which she passed to the groom. He wiped his eyes, handed it back to her, and just as the soloist sang the last note the bride tucked the damp handkerchief back in her bosom and smiled radiantly as though nothing had happened. They needed each other! For this was just the beginning of her ability to bring cheer into his life and perhaps even wipe away many tears. And he was sharing with her a very deep sensitive nature that would enrich her life in years to come. Thank God for opposites!

Beauty or the Beast

Many books have been written to women encouraging them to improve their outward appearance. I feel very strongly that when a woman fully accepts herself as a creation God has made, she will do her very best to prune, trim, manicure and even paint the object of God's love and care. What a pity to see a Christian woman who has developed her inner beauty but has done nothing to the frame she must house it in. On the other hand, how beautiful is the woman who has obeyed the instructions in 1 Peter 3 to develop the hidden "woman" of the heart and then has taken special care to trim and fix up the place in which it dwells.

Recently my husband and I were eating in a restaurant. Our meal was almost ruined when we overheard the man at the table across from us say to his wife, "You look like the devil. You look 85 years old. Why don't you spend five minutes putting on a little make-up and a wig." This man was not right in running his wife down as he did. There were other ways by which he could have accomplished the same thing. But that does not excuse the little lady either. Who knows how many years he had been looking at that tired mess? With all the helps available today, there is no need for a woman to let herself get into this situation. God created things beautiful! I'm sure He enjoys seeing a woman delight in taking care of his handiwork.

Conflict to Contentment

With the blessing and enrichment of opposites comes the necessity for adjustment. Our differences do not need to lead us to the divorce court nor should they be a threat to our marriage. The secret is really how one handles the differences, for good marriages have survived a period of conflict. Those who survive this conflict are the ones who have dealt with their problems prayerfully and are led by the Holy Spirit. Wives, it is of utmost importance to pray four different ways:

First of all, pray about your own attitude and response to the problem. When you examine your heart you may find that you have some confessing to do. You cannot be filled with the Holy Spirit when you are grieving the Spirit by your wrong attitudes or emotions.

Secondly, you must pray for your husband, even in times when you may not feel like praying for him. Nevertheless, ask God to help him to evaluate the situation and recognize his shortcomings.

Thirdly, ask God to lead you in discussing the problem with him. You could ruin everything by discussing it in your own strength and in your own way.

The fourth prayer should be one asking God to fill you with love for your husband so that you can genuinely love him regardless of your differences or his weaknesses. Many times this God-given love will begin to melt away the differences and they will fade into the past.

Not long after our marriage I discovered one of my husband's weaknesses that nobody had warned me about. After a few days of wedded bliss, I detected a habit that was to be repeated day after day. Each morning I would find my husband's socks right where he had removed his shoes the night before. They were never stretched out full length but always rolled up in little round balls—two of them! At the first it was really no problem. I enjoyed picking up his socks, and since I had a strong back, it really didn't hurt me. But the days wore into weeks and the weeks into months. One morning I noticed a little irritation as I picked them up—an irritation not in my back but in my attitude. A few days later the thought crossed my mind, "I wonder who picked up after him before he met me?" It then occurred to me that maybe he really didn't know what the clothes hamper was for. So I introduced him to his special piece of furniture built to house dirty clothes. Nevertheless, I continued to stumble over the dirty socks each morning. Stumble? Yes, because they were growing in size, at least in my mind and attitude. "His back is certainly as strong as mine. He can pick up his own socks," I grumbled.

It is very interesting how a thing so small as two soiled

socks can throw your whole personality off-balance. They caused me to be irritable and critical of many things my husband did. They sparked the fire that caused my mental attitude to go completely out of whack. For when my husband would come home in the evening whistling or singing, I would not see the man who dearly loved me and provided for me. Instead, I would see the wearer of those dirty socks!

On one dull, gloomy day, I picked up the Bible by our night stand and a verse seemed to stand out from all the other verses.

> And whatsoever ye do in word or deed, do all in the name of the Lord Jesus, giving thanks to God and the Father by Him.
>
> *Colossians 3:17*

In my own translation it seemed to say to me, "When you pick up after your husband, even dirty socks, do it in the name of the Lord Jesus, giving thanks to God and the Father by him." I quickly read on,

> Wives, submit yourselves unto your own husbands, as it is fit in the Lord.
>
> *Colossians 3:18*

My eyes dropped down a few verses,

> And whatsoever ye do, do it heartily, as to the Lord, and not unto men; Knowing that of the Lord ye shall receive the reward of the inheritance: for ye serve the Lord Christ.
>
> *Colossians 3:23-24*

I wasn't just picking up dirty socks for my husband; I was serving the Lord Jesus by doing this, so I had to do it heartily as unto Him.

I faced a conflict. My husband may not have even

known about it at the time. (However, I hardly think he couldn't have noticed my rotten attitude.) Under examination I was the one who had to confess and get my attitudes straightened out. Interestingly enough, after I confessed, I truly enjoyed serving the Lord and my husband. It was almost a time of devotion each day as I lovingly picked up those blessed dirty socks. I thanked God for my loving husband who was so faithful and who provided for me and who loved God with all his heart. I knew there were many women who would give anything to be able once again to pick up socks after their husbands. And I was still able! Would you believe that those beautiful dirty socks began to disappear without any word spoken? One day he just decided to be more careful and to pick up after himself. Oh, how I missed those socks. I still get to take them from the clothes hamper and put them into the washing machine. May I do it heartily as unto the Lord!

Should We Have Children?

With all the birth control methods we have today, it is easily possible to go through life without choosing to have children. There was a day when only those who could not conceive did not have babies. The modern trend is to have children only by choice and even then they are scheduled. Some young couples today are so sophisticated, they even try to help determine the sex of the baby before conception.

The days of every little girl having a baby doll and learning to cuddle and mother it are swiftly passing. First Barbie dolls, with mature figures and clothes to match, came on the scene. Ken arrived shortly after and began dating Barbie. Instead of little girls cuddling "make believe'' babies, they were living in a dream world of adults with Barbie and Ken. Recently a TV personality remarked that a popular doll manufacturer was producing Barbie and Ken dolls complete with sex organs. Little girls live these activities through their dolls and begin to think of themselves as sex partners instead of mothers.

Is it any wonder that many teen-age girls do not see themselves as mothers in later years? I hear teen-age girls say, "I never want to have children." On the brighter side, I have one dear friend who has a college-age daughter. Ever since she was very young, she has cuddled dolls and kittens and desired to someday be a mother. Even today when she attends a baby shower, with every little gift that is opened she comments how she would love to have a baby.

The point I am making is that with these changing times and attitudes, we have young married couples who decide they do not want to raise a family. I am not referring to temporary delays but to permanent decisions. Not every couple must have children. However, I do feel that couples who do not pray about it to ascertain God's will may miss out on life's greatest blessing.

In all probability, the temperaments have a lot to do with these attitudes. Probably Sarah Sanguine would want to be a mother since she has so much love to give. She adores children anyway and would love to have her very own. Easy-going Polly Phlegmatic would be willing to go along with her husband's wishes and would be able to adjust to either having or not having children. Martha Melancholy would have a problem deciding if she could really be a good mother. She would want to experience mother-love before she ever conceived. Clara Choleric might have such far-reaching goals that she might feel a child would clutter up her success. At least she would want a limit of one child. Each of these temperaments is influenced, of course, by her partner so the decision might vary and be subject to change.

My husband and I were visiting with several other young couples when, during the course of the evening, my husband asked about their children. They responded that none of them had children. I detected a few glances across the room and a little uneasiness. The subject was dropped for the moment but came to the surface again later. One of the uneasy wives remarked that she never wanted children. Another wife chimed in that she didn't either. My husband was not about to let that die, so he began to question their reasons. They both remarked that they could not love a child sufficiently so they did not want any (both were melancholics). The husbands would have enjoyed being fathers but the wives were very firm. I commented that God gives a woman nine months of preparatory time. It is then that a mother's heart begins to learn to love the little object that is growing within her. The first movements, the increased measurements, the extra heartbeat—all contribute to the mother's growing love for her unborn child. These gals wanted to have that love before pregnancy. Melancholic women want to be assured of and to experience mother-love before they ever conceive. When pregnancy is approached with prayers and anticipation, a mother's heart will be filled with all the love she needs for her baby.

> And God blessed them, and God said unto them, Be fruit-ful, and multiply, and replenish the earth, . . .
>
> *Gen. 1:28a*

The first commandment God gave to man was to multiply and to replenish the earth. Today we have been educated to believe that the earth is overpopulated and we can do our part by not having children. However, our first responsibility is to be obedient to God who created all people and controls the destiny of the world in which we dwell.

As I talk to many of these childless couples, it soon becomes obvious that their true motives are not as noble as they seem on the surface. There seems to be a current of selfishness flowing beneath the most acceptable excuses.

In order to be truly Spirit-controlled, young couples should not make a decision of this importance without first seeking what the Heavenly Father would have them do. Blessing from God must be preceded by obedience.

Communicate! Don't Just Talk

The art of communicating does not mean one must be an excessive talker. Communicating involves listening as well as talking. One dear talkative lady seriously said to me, "I have no trouble communicating," but the truth was that she was dead wrong. What she really meant to say was, "I have no trouble talking." She did all of the talking. Her husband rarely was able to express his views. She knew exactly what she thought but rarely listened to her husband's ideas. He was a great guy. I can just imagine that he had stored up in his mind a wealth of thoughts that he was not allowed to spill out.

Communicating must be two-sided. It must involve listening as well as talking. The lack of proper communication is one of the greatest problems in marriages today.

Women need to pray for a Spirit-controlled tongue to know when to keep silent and when to speak as well as how to say what must be said. How we say something is just as important as what we say.

One of the main ingredients in good communications is love. 1 Corinthians 13 lists many good qualities, but without love they are still nothing. The description of love in this chapter, when used in a marriage, will greatly improve the line of communications between husband and wife. This is truly Spirit-filled communicating.

Love . . . suffereth long

Love . . . is kind

Love . . . envieth not

Love . . . vaunteth not itself

Love . . . is not puffed up

Love . . . does not behave itself unseemly

Love . . . seeketh not her own

Love . . . is not easily provoked

Love . . . thinketh no evil

Love . . . rejoiceth not in iniquity

Love . . . rejoiceth in the truth

Love . . . beareth all things

Love . . . believeth all things

Love . . . hopeth all things

Love . . . endureth all things

Love . . . never faileth.

This love, or communication, is not dependent on the way your husband treats you. It becomes your responsibility to treat him this way. When you accept this responsibility, the lines of communication will be wide open for you.

Right here I would like to insert a thought that has

been shared by many men. Most wives do not realize how easily their remarks can influence the thinking of their husbands. Often just a quick complaint, a criticism, or a negative remark can color the thoughts of a man. One minister-husband remarked that he never allowed his wife to speak a negative remark to him regarding any member of their church. Such a remark so influenced his thoughts toward a person that he was not able to shake it off. Besides, the Bible speaks very clearly about this.

> Speak not evil one of another, brethren. He that speaketh evil of his brother, and judgeth his brother, speaketh evil of the law, and judgeth the law: but if thou judge the law, thou art not a doer of the law, but a judge. *James 4:11*

There have been times when I have carelessly made a comment about someone to my husband. Unknowingly, that remark was stuck in the files of his mind, eventually influencing him for good or bad regarding that person. The Spirit-filled woman must guard her thoughts and remarks lest she bring unnecessary judgment on another individual. We are guilty of praising God one moment and then bringing destruction to another person the next.

> Therewith bless we God, even the Father: and therewith curse we men, which are made after the similitude of God. Out of the same mouth proceedeth blessing and cursing. My brethren, these things ought not so to be. *James 3:9-10*

The Holy Spirit can put controls on our tongues so that our communications may be wise and flavored with love. James continues to say that from the wise only good deeds and comments will pour forth and that if we don't brag about them, then we will be truly wise!

I have learned that on some occasions it is better for

me to communicate with God about a matter and let Him speak to my husband. There are a few subjects that I seem to really mess up when I try to interfere.

A few years ago we were traveling in Europe with two of our children. This was a testing time at best, since we were usually crammed together for many hours a day in a hotel, car, or train. Looking for ways to make the trip enjoyable for everyone, I was concerned that we were omitting an important matter from our fellowship. In the excitement of traveling—with passports, trains, foreign languages, and all the rest—we had neglected to pray together as a family. There were days when I would hint, nag, or even announce that we were struggling because we had not prayed. Then I decided that it would be far more effective and meaningful to the family if my husband would initiate the idea. So I committed it to the Lord, not really expecting much to happen. How surprised I was when somewhere between Vienna and Innsbruck my husband stopped the car and said, "Family, we've been neglecting to have prayer together, and we should not go any further without praying!" What a beautiful sweet spirit of prayer we had and how thankful I was that I had not manipulated it. God had communicated for me!

Proper communication, then, must contain love and wisdom guided by the Holy Spirit. The harvest that you reap will be an honest, peaceable sharing of two hearts and minds.

> But the wisdom from above is first pure, then peaceable, gentle, reasonable, full of mercy and good fruits, unwavering, without hypocrisy. And the seed whose fruit is righteousness is sown in peace by those who make peace.
> *James 3:17-18 (NAS)*

Don't Be Afraid of Submission

The woman who is truly Spirit-filled will want to be totally submissive to her husband. Regardless of what the current trend towards "Women's Lib" advocates, anything which departs from God's design for women is not right. Submission does not mean that she is owned and operated by her husband but that he is the "head" or "manager." A manager knows how to develop and use the gifts in others. This is what God intended the husband to do for the wife. He helps her develop to her greatest potential. He keeps track of the overall picture but puts her in charge of areas where she functions well. This is a truly liberated woman. Submission is God's design for woman. Christ's example teaches that true submission is neither reluctant nor grudging, nor is it a result of imposed authority; it is rather an act of worship to God when it is a chosen, deliberate, voluntary response to a husband.

> Submitting yourselves one to another in the fear of God. Wives, submit yourselves unto your own husbands, as unto the Lord. For the husband is the head of the wife, even as Christ is the head of the church: and he is the savior of the body. Therefore as the church is subject unto Christ, so let the wives be to their own husbands in every thing.
>
> *Ephesians 5:21-24*

Jesus was in total submission to the Father and gave up every right He had. He did not lose His identity. On the contrary, He knew exactly who He was and for what purpose He was on earth. Even though He became a servant in human form, He knew that He was the Son of God, equal with God the Father. In the Godhead there exists perfect unity, equality, and harmony.

Submission is not a status of inferiority. The husband is the head of the wife in the same way the Father is the head of Christ. They are equal and one, but there must be only one leader. God's design is that the husband be in charge. Yet the two are to function together as a team, complementing one another instead of competing with one another.

Some women who act submissive are not submissive in attitude. Women sometimes feel that it is unfair when the husband always gets his way in life.

After speaking at a women's luncheon, a little lady nearing her seventies came up to shake my hand. In a quivering voice she said, "Last week we celebrated our fiftieth wedding anniversary. For all of those years I have *let* my husband be the head of our home. Finally, about a week ago, I decided it was my turn and I took over. It has been miserable and we are both so unhappy. When you spoke today I realized what our trouble is. I am not obeying God." I kissed her and told her to dry away her tears. God saw that she was now willing to submit both in action and in attitude. Christ's example was not an attitude of unfairness felt towards the Father because Christ was the one chosen to become as a servant. The Bible says He humbled himself and was obedient.

> Let this mind be in you, which was also in Christ Jesus: Who, being in the form of God, thought it not robbery to be equal with God: But made himself of no reputation, and took upon him the form of a servant, and was made in the likeness of men: And being found in fashion as a man, he humbled himself, and became obedient unto death, even the death of the cross.
>
> *Phil. 2:5-8*

Then verse 9 goes on to say that God exalted Jesus and gave Him a name which was above every name.

> That at the name of Jesus every knee should bow, of things in heaven, and things in earth, and things under the earth; And that every tongue should confess that Jesus Christ is Lord, to the glory of God the Father.
>
> *Phil. 2:10-11*

Oh, that we could just grasp the attitude in the heart of Jesus—the willingness to be humbled, to be obedient unto death, and to be submissive. It is the principle of losing oneself to find oneself. As the woman humbles herself (dies to self) and submits to her husband (serves him), she begins to find herself within that relationship. A servant is one who gets excited about making somebody else successful. The principles of this world allow a woman to define and insist upon her rights, though in the end she may lose them, but the principles of God are humility and submission. You can live fully by dying to yourself and submitting to your husband.

Recently I had a business contact with a "well-liberated" woman. In the course of conversation a few remarks were made about her marriage and then she blurted, "I guess you know by now that I don't believe in being a clinging vine. The last thing I want is a husband who has to support me!" She described their unusual arrangement, since she seemed to feel that it needed an explanation. Her husband has his job with his own checking account, and she has her position with her own account. They both contribute equal amounts to a joint fund for household expenses. This may sound great on the surface, but underneath there was a steaming bed of coals ready to ignite into a flaming fire. It so happened that she was more successful than he was in the business world; consequently, she could afford a much nicer car than he. Her wardrobe was more elaborate, and she was going on vacation alone this summer because he couldn't afford the kind of trip she could. Our conversation had almost come to a close when she finally said what I had already guessed. "I have lost respect for that man because he has not been more successful!" If we could roll the calendar back a few years, I dare say we would be able to see why he was beaten down and unproductive. She had created this "slob" and now was sick and tired of him. I am sure she had defined her rights and insisted on them and never had considered their working together as a team and building each other up. It wasn't too hard to guess that this husband was a phlegmatic and this wife a "liberated" choleric. In spite of their differences the principles of God could have worked if she had been willing to submit. Now she is so "liberated" that two lonely people go their solitary ways through life. I wonder what that man could have become if she had taken her strengths and humbly submitted herself to him, working with him and letting him be the head!

The wife who truly loves her husband will make his happiness her primary goal. With this kind of motivation, they both are winners in the end!

Just because there is conflict or trouble does not mean that you have to bail out. Divorce is not always the answer. When you have two individuals with two different sets of temperaments you are naturally going to have differences of opinion. The stronger the temperaments, the stronger the conflicts. It takes both partners allowing the Spirit to control their lives to live peaceably and happy. It has been our joy to watch many couples come to this decision in their marriage after much conflict and to see how their lives and marriages have been transformed. With the help of the Holy Spirit you can be married for keeps!

6

LOVE YOUR HUSBAND
TO CHRIST

Where are the Christian men? There have probably been
millions of Christian women married to unbelieving husbands since the history of the church. It seems after
every lecture I am confronted with at least five or six
who ask for special prayer for their partners. This group
of women needs to have an unusual amount of God-given
love flowing through them. There are times when one of
these women may wonder how she can continue; surely
it would take heavenly grace and divine wisdom to live
with some of the men I have heard women tell about. But
God is so faithful! Nothing is impossible! He loves with
an everlasting love and His heart is grieved over an un-

saved partner. After all, He died for the soul of that man.

Live a Godly Life

Many husbands have been won to Christ by the wife's constant and faithful loving attitude toward him. A wife should not try to change her husband; she must learn to accept him just as he is. Some husbands become very demanding and somewhat unreasonable as the Holy Spirit convicts them. This is a time of suffering and trial for the family, especially the wife. He needs to be surrounded with a spirit of prayer and understanding; she needs the infilling of the Holy Spirit to remain steady and calm. It is God's design that a wife submit to her husband even though he is not a believer.

> In the same way, you wives, be submissive to your own husbands so that even if any of them are disobedient to the word, they may be won without a word by the behavior of their wives, as they observe your chaste and respectful behavior.
>
> *1 Peter 3:1-2 (NAS)*
>
> But let it be the hidden person of the heart, with the imperishable quality of a gentle and quiet spirit, which is precious in the sight of God. For in this way in former times the holy women also, who hoped in God, used to adorn themselves, being submissive to their own husbands.
>
> *1 Peter 3:4-5 (NAS)*

Understand him. Your unbelieving husband has a great need for understanding and companionship—don't compete with him. He certainly doesn't need a nagging wife; he needs a positive and creative woman by his side. Try to understand what makes him angry or happy and what causes him to suffer. How can you best encourage him? Don't discuss his problems outside of your home. And most of all, don't constantly remind your husband about God—instead remind God about your husband.

Please him. The wife of the unsaved husband should be the best homemaker in town. She should cook to please her husband. Her housework should be bathed with love and prayer. Some husbands become rather critical of their Christian wives. It is her responsibility to do all she can to please him, and in so doing she will be a credit to her husband. More important than what she does is the attitude in which she does it. She should be pleasant, a joy to be around.

Respect him. You need to be extremely careful that you are obedient and respectful to your husband. There may be some rare instances when you cannot be submissive or obedient to your husband, but that is only when you are asked to do something that is absolutely contrary to the Scriptures. There are very few examples of this— adultery, lying, stealing, etc. Too many times women use the reasoning that the Lord has led them to go contrary to their husbands without a definite command from the Scriptures. This may mean that you have to give up your involvement in a Bible class or even your church attendance. Remember, your obedience and submission when done in the right spirit will do more to win him to Christ than your attendance at a Bible study.

Examine yourself. Do you preach at him? Can you entrust your husband to God and leave the consequences of his actions to your Heavenly Father? Have you trained your children to respect their father? Are you so active in your church that you are away from home a good bit of the time? Have you been critical and cold towards him? You may need to confess and ask forgiveness from your husband for your wrong attitude and actions.

Have you ever thought of the other side of submission? So many women get "testy" when discussing that subject. All they can think of is their downtrodden rights. Has it ever occurred to you that God would never have asked you to submit to your husband unless he had a need for your respect and admiration? The most frustrated men we deal with are not vocational or educational failures, they are men whose wives do not respect them by submitting themselves to them. In many cases, the man is worthy of his wife's respect, but she is just so domineering she refuses to submit. Both are losers in such a marriage!

My husband and I were able to observe a godly woman who literally loved her husband to the Lord. She first began to attend church all by herself. She slipped into the service and out again without lingering so it was difficult to get acquainted with her. We later learned that she attended our early service and left immediately after so she could be home in time to serve her husband breakfast just as he was getting out of bed. She spent every Sunday with him, "fitting into his plans." This woman was a silent worshipper. She dearly loved the Lord yet when asked to teach a Sunday School class, graciously refused. Her refusal did not reflect her lack of desire to teach but her priority at that time of being a godly wife and partner to her unsaved husband. She declined joining the church without her husband, since she felt that they were to be united even in church membership. Whether or not she was right in this matter, she still had a beautiful spirit and a desire to be a godly woman.

We watched her continue like this as a faithful, serving, and submissive wife for almost seven years. One Easter Sunday her husband announced that he was going to get up a little earlier than usual and attend church with his wife. This was all his idea and just the beginning of a new life for him. Shortly after, he invited the Lord Jesus into his heart and that couple became one in Christ. Today they are faithful church members and serve on various boards of the church. This lady can look back on those years of waiting and silent worship without regret. She had not nagged or preached or deserted him for church services; instead, she had just lived a beautiful, consistent life before him.

7

YOU MARRIED
HIS PROFESSION

"Fitting in with your husband's plans" may mean you have him only part-time because of his profession. I have listened to the stories of wives of servicemen, doctors, ministers, politicians, sales executives, etc., and they all sound very much the same: "My husband is gone so much of the time, I am left to raise the kids and run the house by myself." There seems to be a mixture of loneliness, self-pity, bitterness, and depression in the cries of these women. They feel trapped!

A visit with a Congressman's wife in Washington, D.C., revealed that she had suffered severely when he first took office. He was dedicated to his new profession and earnestly tried to do a good job for his country. Naturally, that meant long hours each day at the office and several extended trips back to his constituents. She had built quite a case, constantly asking herself what she was doing in Washington. Even the task of carrying out the trash, which he had always done previously, was a daily reminder to her that she was left alone to run a large house and to raise three children with only a part-time father and husband. Her self-pity grew to the extent that she began to let her appearance run down. She wallowed in her lonely, depressed state. The short hours her husband did spend with her were spent listening to a complaining, critical woman who looked like she had lost her comb and mirror. Conditions grew from bad to worse until she was considering moving the children back to her home state. But God intervened. She was invited to a Bible study class in Washington where she met other wives of politicians and government workers who were radiantly happy and fulfilled women. What did they have that made them so different? They had to live with a husband who was often away from home just as she did, but they seemed to be able to handle it so much better. She was introduced to Jesus Christ and accepted the One who is able to make the difference. Through all this she learned that proper attitudes toward her husband and his profession would change her outlook on life. She told me that she began to count the blessings, for there was much she could be thankful for. Several months had already passed when I first met her. My initial impression of her was that she was a glowing, joyful person. The Holy Spirit made the difference! I am sure that her husband is a much better Congressman because of the spirit of the woman behind him. She has become a real helpmeet.

The same can be said of wives whose husbands are doctors, ministers, or in any other line of work. Husbands can be much more successful and at peace with themselves when they have a wife behind them who has a Spirit-filled attitude toward her husband's profession and is willing "to fit in with their husband's plans."

I believe that I can write on this from personal experience. My husband has traveled much, holding family seminars and prophetic meetings across the U.S.A. When our children were young, it was difficult for me to accept his periodic absences. I could dwell on these negatives the entire time he was away, and by the time he returned, he had a real depressed tyrant on his hands. After one of his meetings away, I received a letter from a lady who had been especially blessed in this meeting. Her letter went something like this,

> Dear Mrs. LaHaye,
> I do not know you, but I wish to thank you for sharing your husband with so many other people. It must be difficult for you to be alone so much of the time. I am sure that you were home praying for him that God would use him in a mighty way. [Groan] My heart was so blessed by his messages, and God used him to help me work out a very serious problem in our family. You will be greatly rewarded for your kindness and faithfulness to our Heavenly Father!
> Signed

Little did she know that I was not home praying; rather I was complaining and griping. But God used that precious lady to prick my conscience, and I realized how I was missing out. I did not share the blessings! I became my husband's greatest prayer warrior after that. It is surprising how our spirit changes when we are praying instead of complaining. From that day on I became a part of his ministry and shared in the blessings. Today I am traveling with my husband and speaking in the Family Life Seminar ministry that I was negative toward in the beginning.

A leading woman's magazine told the story of a senator's wife who was legally separated from her husband for three years because of the loneliness of his profession. She stated that she came back to him because she learned that in spite of all their differences in temperament and goals, she was never going to find another man that she admired or respected more than this man. There was no indication in the article that she was a believer in Christ. If she could come to that decision without Christ, how much more readily can we with Christ's help.

When we dwell on the positive and learn to accept things we cannot change, we will be one step higher up the ladder toward happiness. The results of the Spirit-filled life will be joy, peace, longsuffering, and a singing, thankful heart!

Lila Trotman—wife of Dawson Trotman, who was president of the Navigators before his death—once stated, "Your husband will never truly be yours until you have first given him back to God. He is yours only when you are willing to let him go wherever God calls him and do what God wants him to do. You must always be willing to let God be first in his life." Remember, he belongs first to God, then to you.

8

MENOPAUSE
IS NOT THE END

This change does not mean the end of living! Many women are depressed when they are faced with the fact that they can no longer bear children—not that they really want babies at that age, but it brings to a close the period in their life when they can reproduce.

Other doors seem to close for women about the same time. The challenge and opportunity to help build their children's lives may end as the last child probably will soon be "closing" the door of home to go out on his own. Employed women may see their jobs "closing" in on them and feel threatened by younger women. Looking in the mirror, women often see the door of their youth "closing." They may even entertain the thought that their sexual enjoyment with their husbands is coming to a close. This is not generally true, but many do experience such difficulty. A medical doctor can usually remedy this with proper treatment.

Every woman would like her menopause period and the years that follow to be great and memorable days in her mature life. There is relief from the fear of pregnancy, freedom from the burden of caring for small children, and an end of troubles with the distress of menstruation. Some women have reported that they have been relieved from a lot of aches and pains and that they have more energy than ever before. Many women report that menopause actually improves their sex life because they no longer face the fear of pregnancy.

A healthy mental attitude is very important during this period of life. Don't go into it remembering that Aunt Matilda claimed it was the darkest days of her life. Approach it positively with other interests in life besides, "How do I feel today?" Too much self-examination of your physical health at this time will surely produce new ailments and undue concern.

> Be anxious for nothing; but in everything by prayer and supplication with thanksgiving let your requests be made known unto God.
>
> *Philippians 4:6*

In spite of the fact that one era may be closing, remember that a new one is opening up for you. You may now have time for the interests that you have always wanted to develop but never had time. You can draw on your maturity and experience of life. Capabilities that may have been dormant can now be pulled out and put to good use. There is a satisfaction in knowing that you have completed your responsibilities in one phase of life and now are stepping out into a new era.

My own dear mother has stepped forth through this new gate opened for her and is blossoming into full bloom. She had not been employed outside of her home since she was twenty-five years old. Now well into her seventies, she has a spirit of new energy; many of her aches and pains have subsided, and she is employed in the mail room of a Christian organization. Her doctor reports that she is better today than she was ten years ago. She is living and fulfilling a second chapter of her life.

A medical doctor has related the following information that I consider important enough to pass on to you. During menopause most women have a tendency to spread out in the hip and thigh area. The wise woman will diet and engage in regular physical exercise during these years to help control any weight gain. After the menopause period has passed, the chances are rather good that if she has controlled her hip measurements she will have it licked for life. On the other hand, if she does not conquer the bulges, they will be with her forevermore.

No, menopause is not the end! It is merely a step up the ladder of life. For the woman who is totally committed to Jesus Christ, each step higher up the ladder will become more precious and fulfilling. The Holy Spirit will help you to become mature gracefully. Your mental attitude toward menopause can make the difference between your last half of life being a drudgery or a delight.

9

THE TOTAL HOMEMAKER

Most women are homemakers for at least a major part of their life, either by choice or of necessity. If they have not married, they may be making a home for an elderly parent, a roommate, or even for themselves. The married woman becomes a homemaker for her husband and her family. I'm a bit weary of hearing women say, "I'm just a homemaker." God created women to be helpers, and where better could we begin than right in our own home? The virtuous woman described in Proverbs 31 is one who "looketh well to the ways of her household."

Head of Homemaking Department

Happy, successful homemaking will depend on the

proper attitudes and priorities in your home.

> And whatever ye do in word or deed, do all in the name of the Lord Jesus, giving thanks to God and the Father by him.
>
> *Colossians 3:17*

There were times—yes, many times—in the earlier days of our marriage when my housework was not done with an attitude of giving thanks nor was it done in the name of the Lord Jesus. In my case it was not the major problems that succeeded in wearing me down; it was the smoldering resentment caused from the endless little tasks that had to be repeated over and over again and seemed so futile. Day after day I would perform the same routine procedures: picking up dirty socks, hanging up wet towels, closing closet doors, turning off lights that had been left on, creating a path through the clutter of toys. These jobs seemed so unproductive, and they were performed with drudgery. With this kind of an attitude, resentment mounted and in turn produced depression—I truly was "just a housewife!" When your attitude is wrong, it causes you to also get your priorities out of line.

This was not what God wanted for me. He had called me to be a helper in our home, and He had made me "Head" of the Homemaking Department. His instructions for the job were found in the Bible:

> And whatever ye do, do it heartily as to the Lord and not unto men, knowing that of the Lord ye shall receive the reward of the inheritance; for ye serve the Lord Christ.
>
> *Colossians 3:23-24*

I was to do my job heartily as unto the Lord, for I was serving the Lord Christ! After all, our home belonged to

God. We had dedicated it to Him and asked Him to be the head of it. God had made my husband the head of certain other departments and assigned me to be head of homemaking. Nowhere could I work for a greater boss or have any more responsible position. I was head hostess in charge of His home, and this place was to reflect a godly abode showing order, love, and contentment.

In my kitchen hangs a plaque on which is inscribed a poem, written by an author I do not know, which reads:

Kitchen Prayer

Lord of all pots and pans and things,
　　since I've not time to be
A saint by doing lovely things
　　or watching late with Thee

Or dreaming in the dawn light
　　or storming heaven's gates,
Make me a saint by getting meals
　　and washing up the plates.

Warm all the kitchen with Thy love
　　and light it with Thy peace.
Forgive me all my worrying
　　and make my grumbling cease.
Thou who didst love to give men food
　　in room or by the sea,
Accept the service that I do;
　　I do it unto Thee.

When this spirit is reflected in your homemaking, it will not make a difference which temperament you are. The careless sanguine will realize a new sense of responsibility and put order into her home. The dominant choleric woman will develop a softness, and her home will abound with love. The cautious phlegmatic gal will certainly be more motivated to do the job before her, and the grumbling melancholic will have a more happy and contented spirit.

You must ask yourself what the object of your housekeeping is. Is it for your own satisfaction? Is it to meet the standards of your neighbors and friends who may drop in? Or is it to maintain a comfortable place of refuge for those you love and want to serve?

Many homemakers escape the reality of their position by reading novels, listening to daytime TV serials, running to the neighbors, or talking for hours on the telephone. They are victims of TV commercials that make the American homemaker appear as though she had neither brains nor common sense. The Spirit-filled homemaker will be hesitant to identify with this figure.

Temperamental Decorating

Your home and how it is decorated represents you as a happy, contented homemaker or as a disgruntled I-couldn't-care-less lady of the house. It does not need to have elaborate and expensive furnishings. It is possible to give it a warm, loving, cared-for appearance and still be conservative in cost. Use a little imagination, a paint brush, sewing machine, and some other do-it-yourself projects, and notice the difference it makes.

How you decorate your home will probably reveal something about your temperament or perhaps your husband's, depending on who makes the choices. A very generalized summary of colors and temperaments goes something like this:

> Melancholic—subdued winter colors: muted shades of brown, black, grey, wine.
>
> Phlegmatic—soft, spring colors: pastels of green, yellow, pink, blue

Choleric—warm autumn colors: gold, brown, burgundy, soft orange

Sanguine—bright, vivid colors: red, bright orange, green, yellow

Remember these color preferences are not absolute because you have a combination of temperaments that causes several colors to blend together. Most of all, your home with its colors, designs, and total look should bear evidence that Christ dwells in the hearts of the people who live there.

Secret of Hospitality

Don't just exist in your home; take time to live there! Be hospitable! The art of being hospitable does not demand elaborate preparations and costly goodies; just be yourself and be friendly.

What is the purpose of hospitality? The main purpose is not to feed your guests—they can eat at home. More important than the food is your willingness to share a part of yourself—your love, your kindness, your generosity—and your guests can only get this from you! Be ready to listen to them, really listen, for they may be reaching out to you for comfort or friendship or perhaps help during a time of loneliness and struggle.

I used to have the mistaken idea that being hospitable meant being a slave and nearly killing myself in preparations, so when the time came for the guests, I felt more like going up to bed than going to answer the door. "But a lover of hospitality, a lover of good men, soberminded, just, holy, temperate" is what Titus 1:8 commands us to be. Some of the most memorable examples of hospitality that I have experienced have been with people who were delighted to share themselves and what they had without too much advance notice. They had a wonderful gift of making people feel at ease and very welcome in their home. When the hostess is tense, the guests will usually sense this and be tense also. In contrast to this, we were once invited to a lovely home for dinner by very wonderful people. However, the hostess was not relaxed or at ease, and even though she had prepared a very elegant meal that was served in a nearly perfect manner, we could all sense her tension. She was so determined that the evening be flawless that she put everyone under a strain. It would have been far more enjoyable if she had just done her best and then become flexible, relaxed, and willing to share herself with us. Sometimes a not-so-perfect evening can be more delightful than a totally perfect one.

Being hospitable does not mean showing off your lovely home or displaying your ability in the kitchen. It means showing the warmth and friendship of yourself and your family. It also is not necessary to serve a seven-course dinner to be hospitable. Your fellowship over a cookie and a cup of coffee can be very effective when shared with a genuine welcome spirit.

Hospitality sometimes means going outside of your home to be hospitable—maybe taking a hot casserole supper to your sick neighbor or perhaps calling on the widow who needs a friend in her loneliness. Don't be afraid to give and give and give.

> Be not forgetful to entertain strangers, for thereby some have entertained angels unawares.
>
> *Hebrews 13:2*

Root of All Evil

"The LOVE of money is the root of all evil." The successful Christian homemaker will not be guilty of loving money to the extent that she gets her priorities out of order and neglects those things that are of true value. The desire for things such as a better home, a newer car, many clothes, or nicer furniture, etc. can very subtly draw the homemaker into a discontented and covetous position. Money cannot buy happy home relationships, and if having one's desires met means that she must leave her home and go to work, then she probably should examine her priorities and values. The Spirit-filled woman will have a greater desire to please God in this area than her desire for material things. Thus, she can seek His leading and keep her priorities in right order.

Homemaking Temperaments

The following is a summary of how the different temperaments would score in the Homemaking Department. There may be overlaps and you may find yourself in two or three of these categories since no one is wholly one temperament.

Martha Melancholy—Martha will usually excel as a good cook, a clever interior decorator, or an antique lover; she is also able to produce do-it-yourself artistic touches for her home. Her moodiness keeps her from being too hospitable.

Polly Phlegmatic—She is a good, all-round homemaker, who is usually faithful and consistent. She has the potential of being a gourmet cook and a good seamstress because of her great patience. Probably Polly will be a slow worker but nice to be around.

Clara Choleric—This one is great at entertaining and can do just about anything she sets her mind to. However, though her home will be well-organized she is not a natural homemaker. Her home is a great place to look at but usually is not a good place in which to live.

Sarah Sanguine—Sarah is very hospitable and neighborly because of her warm love for people. She loves to eat and is usually a good cook. Her home may not always be too neat, but she will share anything she has with others.

Because of the fruit of the Holy Spirit each temperament can overcome any homemaking weaknesses by having total commitment and proper attitudes. It isn't the woman's taste in decorating and color arrangement that makes a home peaceful and charming; it is the woman herself.

10

WIVES FIRST, MOTHERS SECOND

The role of mother is important but should never be put ahead of the role of wife. After all, most women are wives from forty to sixty years, whereas they are mothers (during their children's live-at-home years) for only eighteen to twenty-eight years. The Bible emphasizes the husband-wife role in contrast to man-made religions which stress the parent-child and father-mother relationships.

When a young mother spends most of her time and energy with her children, her husband begins to feel neglected and jealous. When a little baby cries out, the mother is quick to respond; but many a husband cries out in his own way, and his wife does not even hear him. Sometimes a wife will also feel like crying out for attention or understanding, but she should not expect her husband to hear her unless she has already been responsive to his silent pleas. God has given her a mother instinct for this, so it will, of course, come more naturally for her than for him. When she ignores her husband's cries, resentment and unhappiness sets in between them, thereby creating an insecure atmosphere for the whole family. Children can readily sense happiness and love, and they respond to it. A popular speaker on family living has said that the greatest gift you can give a child is to love his father.

After the children are grown, there will be a period of twenty to thirty years when the husband and wife live alone. Usually about one half of a marriage will be spent without children. So husband and wife had better be friends! Many divorces occur between partners who are forty years of age or older simply because time was not spent during their early years together in developing a lasting friendship. The time to lay the foundation for that lasting happiness is while the children are still at home. Every wife needs to develop a true friendship with her husband. So, gals, be a nice person to have around because you are going to see a lot of each other. The woman who is first a wife and then a mother has laid the foundation for lasting marital happiness.

To maintain a lasting relationship flavored with peace and harmony, the Christian wife and mother needs a personal experience and a daily walk with Jesus Christ. God's divine plan for husband and wife relationships is a triangle of fellowship.

The husband must have nothing between the Lord and himself—the line of communication and love must be open. Likewise, the wife must have the right relationship with Jesus Christ. When husband and wife are in proper fellowship with the Lord, then the absolute result is a good relationship with one another. When there is a disruption in that fellowship, then it is almost sure that one of them has had a break in their communication with Jesus Christ.

> But if we walk in the light as He is in the light, we have fellowship one with another; and the blood of Jesus Christ, his Son, cleanseth us from all sin.
>
> *1 John 1:7*

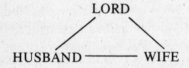

When this triangle is functioning openly and freely, it provides a solid foundation on which to begin a Christian family.

Blessings or Blight

Some time ago I heard a minister state that a blessing was something that drew us closer to God. Couples pray for the blessing of a baby, but if that child does not draw them closer to God, then it becomes a blight. What a tragedy that something so adorable and innocent as a baby could become a wedge between the parents and God. Parents sometimes develop wrong attitudes and get their priorities out of line. I have seen young parents drop out of church and its activities when a baby comes on the scene, and they become spiritually bankrupt. If only they could realize that they need God's blessing and divine wisdom even more after a family is begun. God entrusts parents with the lives of His little ones so that they can grow physically and spiritually. He has a plan for each one of their lives. How dare we interfere and cause that little child to start off down the wrong pathway of life. Within that little baby's body is the capacity for a full-blown man or woman who will do a work for God. After all, God sent a baby when He had a job that needed to be accomplished—His name was Jesus!

Trials and Triumphs

There is no other area of life that has more trials yet provides such great blessings as parenthood. Being a parent can bring us to the depths of sorrow and the heights of joy. We can laugh and cry, or we can panic and despair.

During a child's early years, the important role for the mother is that of servant. Nine months of waiting for the blessed event are rewarded with interrupted sleep at night, daily loads of laundry, constant care, and loss of freedom almost to the point where the mother feels she is a prisoner in her own home. The joys come when that helpless creature rewards mother for all her efforts by a half smile from his little mouth. That is just the beginning of an endless cycle of serving and rewards, serving and rewards.

From the very beginning the mother becomes a teacher without being fully aware of it. Her area of specialization ranges all the way from teaching that little darling to take food from a spoon to teaching the teen-age lady how to make a cheese souffle or the teen-age fellow how to launder his own shirts.

An extra portion of patience is needed by every mother during these teaching training years. There are going to be moments of frustration, sighs of disgust, or even thoughts of "Why did I ever become a parent?" It will happen to any mother who breathes. The secret is to not allow it to linger until it turns into self-pity and resentment.

One such experience happened to my married daughter who has two children, aged three and one. She had just disciplined the three-year-old and sent her to her bedroom weeping and wailing. The telephone rang, and as she grabbed it to say "Hello," the doorbell chimes sounded. Trying desperately to keep calm, she struggled to hear who her telephone caller was over the yelling of her three-year-old. It was just about that moment that she glanced down the hall and noticed her one-year-old having a joyful time playing in the toilet. At that point she lost her cool. The only natural thing to do was to sit on the floor and cry. But the world doesn't end at a time like this. If you find yourself in a similar situation, wait until you finally come to yourself, and then attend to the urgent matters at hand with a prayer on your lips that the Lord will forgive you and help you through the next few moments. This is a great time to quote a verse of Scripture aloud as you rush to answer the door or grab the baby from the toilet bowl.

These times are bound to happen in every home. Our daughter-in-law and son have one little boy two years old. One Sunday Kathy was baby-sitting this two-year-old as well as our other daughter's two children. The three ranged in age from one to three, and that makes for a full-time job even when everything is running smoothly. On this particular day the one-year-old had just awakened from a nap and wanted to be held. While Kathy was holding the crying child the telephone rang. It was her dentist, calling back to give her some important information on the treatment of her two-year-old's front teeth that had been chipped during a fall a few days earlier. As she stood in front of the window talking on the phone, she noticed that her two-year-old had somehow opened the gate to the swimming pool area and was moving as fast as his little legs could carry him. Where was the three-year-old? What was the dentist saying? Her mind whirled as she caught a glimpse of the three-year-old out in front where the Sunday afternoon traffic was heavy. I cannot fill in all the details of that story because I don't know where she ran first, but I am happy to report that everything turned out well. Kathy probably had a nervous stomach or a splitting headache for some time afterwards, but when she regained her composure and spent a moment with the Lord, she was back to normal again.

After each such experience, the wise mother will find a time to be alone with God, even if it is later in the evening when everybody is tucked in bed. Tap the sources of strength available to you through the Holy Spirit. This is a time of rebuilding and reinforcing to prepare you for the events of the next day.

Teens in Trouble

"Dear God, how could it happen to my child?" This is

the cry of many parents who are confronted with the cold reality that their child is in deep trouble. "Where did we go wrong?" or "If we could just live those days over again."

Children do not need or want parents to be their chums. It is easier to be a friend, a buddy, or even a dictator than to be a mature, level-headed parent. But the teen-ager needs parents who have convictions and the strength to enforce them during these years of temptations and trouble.

Good relationships are essential to help stabilize and salvage the teen-ager when the going gets rough. A sound relationship is built by beginning at an early age. Accept the child as a person on his own, a little individual. You must establish a clear-cut outline of standards and at the same time maintain an honest, open relationship in which feelings are accepted and spirits are humbled as together divine guidance is sought for each day's needs. Consistency in conduct and requirements are necessary. Proper discipline will bring lasting results to both the child and parent.

When relationships break down and a child gets into trouble, parents begin to fret, "If only we had known, we could have done things differently!" A family counselor on the West Coast says there are signals in childhood to watch for, the first sign being a pulling away from the values of the family and society. The child will ignore or scoff at the Christian influence in the family and will take no part in spiritual activities. Rebellion is not unusual in adolescence, but the radical rejection of the usual value system is a definite warning. If rebellion is handled properly, it is not destructive. But if it turns into a battle for power, someone has to win and someone has to lose.

Mothers and fathers must face these problems as mature adults. There are too many children trying to bring up children; when trouble hits, such parents fall apart and want to run from it. Teens in trouble have disrupted many homes and broken many hearts.

Recently the *U.S. News and World Report* ("As Parents' Influence Fades—Who's Raising the Children?" 27 October 1975, p. 41) listed some of the following statistics:

> By the age of 18, one out of 9 youths ends in juvenile court.
>
> Approximately 10 percent of all school-age children have some degree of mental and emotional trouble. Drug abuse and alcoholism among teens are becoming serious public health problems.
>
> One out of 10 American girls by the age of 17—married or not—is a mother in spite of the availability of many birth-control helps.
>
> Over 1 million (mostly middle-class) young Americans run away from home each year.

A local newspaper reported the following information on drug and alcohol users from a survey of high school and college students across the country ("Drug Sampling Reported High Among Students," *The San Diego Union*, Sept. 27, 1975, p. A-12, cols. 1-2):

> 48% of high school students have experimented with drugs at least once or twice.
>
> 64% of college students have experimented with drugs at least once or twice.
>
> 26% of high school students consider themselves regular drug users.

41% of college students consider themselves regular drug users.

66% of the abusers and 37% of the users have run away from home.

36% of the abusers and 16% of the users have failed courses at school.

The survey concluded with the information that 35% of all students do not use drugs because they are "moral nonusers." They identify with "traditional values and lifestyles" and believe drugs represent a violation of that standard. There is a lot to be said for teaching your children proper values and standards. It may pay off high dividends when the teen-ager is confronted with these temptations. These statistics lose their value unless they can be a reminder to parents to be consistent in teaching proper standards for living. When a parent is inclined to let down and go easy in training and discipline, a look at statistics like these may help to prod him on. This is an area of parenthood that seems to be an impossible task without the help of the Holy Spirit. Parents need to have an extra portion of long-suffering, gentleness, and self-control.

My phone awakened me one Saturday morning. It was a mother calling from across the United States. The hour was early, but when people have problems they are not usually too conscious of the time. In her distress, she shared how her thirteen-year-old son was involved in much trouble. Through her tears she told me how rebellious he was. The signs started showing a few years before when he began to reject the values of the family. They were church-going people but were misguided into believing they should not make him attend with them.

And that was the beginning of his downhill slide. One thing led to another until she was on the phone crying her heart out to me: "Oh, how much easier it would have been if we had just made him attend church the first time he didn't want to!" I prayed with the lady over the phone, though there were very few words of comfort I could share with her—it was truly a black picture. But through prayer I asked that the Heavenly Father comfort the heart of this broken mother and give her wisdom to know the next step to take. Only God could make anything beautiful out of this tragic situation. The time to act is before you get to the place where this dear mother was.

> Chasten thy son while there is hope, and let not the soul spare for his crying.
>
> *Proverbs 19:18*

Dr. Henry Brandt, Christian psychologist, tells the story about his teen-age daughter. She decided one night that she didn't like church and wasn't going. He informed her that she was going and even had to help her put her shoes on and get into the car. Needless to say, she went. And even though she went unhappily, the problem was nipped in the bud before it developed into a tragic situation. Today the Brandts have a lovely Christian daughter in whom they delight. Remember, God has promised:

> Train up a child in the way he should go, and when he is old, he will not depart from it.
>
> *Proverbs 22:6*

Mom (and Dad), one of the greatest things needed in raising children is wisdom. God has promised to give sound wisdom to the righteous and those that walk uprightly. Ask for wisdom for today's needs.

He layeth up sound wisdom for the righteous; he is a shield to those who walk uprightly. He keepeth the paths of justice and preserveth the way of his saints.

Proverbs 2:7-8

Delivered and Delighted

The Lord is my rock, and my fortress, and my deliverer.

2 Samuel 22:2

. . . He delivereth me because he delighted in me.

2 Samuel 22:20b

As for God, his way is perfect; the word of the Lord is tried. He is a shield to all them that trust in him.

2 Samuel 22:31

God is my strength and power; and he maketh my way perfect.

2 Samuel 22:33

As I look back on the past twenty-seven years I have been a mother, there have been many instances when the Lord has been the deliverer for my children:

There was the day our five-year-old son was struck in the head by a moving car, and both wheels ran over his legs. After 55 x-rays the doctors could not believe that he had no broken bones, just a mild concussion. The Lord delivered him!

On another occasion our four-year-old daughter was surviving in a hospital bed with the help of an oxygen tent. The doctors had informed us they had done all they possibly could. Two of the deacons from our church joined us around her bed for prayer and committed her to the Lord. The Lord delivered her!

At age three another daughter suffered from a severe case of measles and complications. For several hours her temperature ranged from 105° to 106°, and we were warned that this could cause permanent brain damage. Once again God intervened and today she and her husband are in Christian work. The Lord delivered her!

When our son was drafted into the Army, he was selected because of his excellent marksmanship to attend a specialized school for sniper training. His father pleaded with God not to allow this great specimen of a young man to come home with only half a body. Through very miraculous circumstances he was taken out of the sniper school and given an eight-hour-a-day desk job in Hawaii! The Lord delivered him!

This same son went through many days of "trying his wings" and questioning his relationship to Jesus Christ. In the Army he was confronted with new temptations and a way of life that was foreign to him. Because of the faithful prayers of a godly girlfriend and his parents, he survived none the worse. The Lord delivered him!

Today this son and his wife have a beautiful Christian home and are a testimony for Jesus Christ to their neighbors and friends. When your children get to the age that they want to take another look at Jesus Christ—an examining and questioning look—leave them to the Lord. Trust God to direct their thoughts and to guide their feet down the path in which you have trained them as a child (another reason why parents must be consistent with their training in the early years). The Lord has promised to be our deliverer because He delights in us.

These children have been entrusted into our care for approximately eighteen to twenty-one years. When we follow God's plan and draw upon Him for strength and wisdom, parenthood can be one of life's most rewarding experiences. I have a little file of special letters my children have written to me over the years. There is a letter from my sixth-grader when he was away at camp: "Just wanted to let you know, Mother, how much I love you." Another precious keepsake is a handwritten note from one of them who was traveling with a youth travel camp: "Tonight, Mom, I rededicated my life to the Lord. Thank you for praying." These are only a few of my jewels that I treasure greatly and will keep forever. These are just a few of the joys of being a mother.

11

WHEN YOUR CHILDREN MARRY

The Challenge of Being a Mother-in-law

The Spirit-filled woman will be a Spirit-filled mother-in-law. There is something about being a mother-in-law that exposes the real traits within a woman. If she is naturally a selfish and possessive person, that is the kind of mother-in-law she will be. If she is a loving, gracious, and kind woman, it will be easy for her to be a Spirit-filled mother-in-law.

A well-known marriage counselor states that most mother-in-law problems stem from the conflict of two women who are both in love with and interested in the same man. One of the most important factors in a mother-in-law's ability to accept her son's new wife is her own relationship to her husband. If she has a wholesome love relationship with her husband, then it is easy for her to welcome her son's wife into her family as a daughter. If, however, she has had a poor love relationship with her partner and, as is often the case, has developed an inordinate and overly possessive love relationship with her son, it is almost certain she will have difficulty accepting his bride. In the instance where the mother-in-law has lived without a husband for many years, it is quite possible that the son has been a "stand-in" companion for her to lean on for comfort and advice. It may then be difficult for her to fade into the background and allow the new wife to be his companion.

A mother with such a smothering love is not aware of the problem until she finds herself competing with another woman for the love of her son. Whenever such competition occurs, the mother-in-law should realistically face the fact that she is 100 percent wrong, because the Bible says:

> For this cause [marriage] shall a man leave his father and mother, and cleave to his wife.
>
> *Mark 10:7*

Many a mother fails to realize that once her son and daughter-in-law leave the church as husband and wife, her role in her son's life will never again be the same. Previous to this time she has likely been the most dominant female figure in her son's life. Now the best thing she can do is to entrust him to his bride and both of them into the hands of God, while she studiously becomes less and less of a present influence on him. In fact, she should be advised to use her mature, womanly talents to support and exalt this young wife to her son.

We have a beautiful picture of the unselfish mother-in-law's attitude in the life of John the Baptist. When he met Christ he said, "He must increase and I must decrease." Williams' translation interprets it, "He must grow greater and greater and I less and less." Since a husband and wife, according to Ephesians 5, are a symbol of Christ and the Church, it reasonably follows that a mother-in-law corresponds with the "friend of the bridegroom." The attitude of a mother toward the new woman in her son's life should be, in the words of John, "She must grow greater and greater (in the eyes of the son) and I (his mother) less and less."

Admittedly, this is hard for a mother at first, but it pays big dividends in the love relationship she builds between herself and those two young people. This investment will repay her with a continuing relationship with her son and gain for her the love of a daughter.

To accept her child's choice of partner is very important for a mother, even when she may not have approved of the marriage. She must be willing to forgive and forget and then to love and accept them both.

> Be ye kind one to another, tenderhearted, forgiving one another, even as God, for Christ's sake, hath forgiven you.
>
> *Ephesians 4:32*

The mother-in-law can add to the happiness and contentment of the young couple by being understanding and not demanding. One of the greatest problems in this area is how and where to spend holidays. The mother can cause undue hardship and turmoil in this new home by planning the holidays according to her own desires with little or no consideration for the son and daughter. In doing this, she risks ruining a good relationship with both of them. How much better it would be to make the times when they are together so enjoyable that the couple would desire to spend part of their holidays as she wishes. The fellowship on a particular holiday is not worth losing the relationship of two young people for life. There are bound to be some pressures that cause parents to be left out of the couple's plans on certain holidays, but parents should make it easy on the young people by joyfully accepting whatever opportunities they can to be together.

Begin Early To Avoid In-law Problems

A good foundation can be laid long before the wedding takes place. Both families can be brought together during the dating days and before the engagement. Planning the events of a wedding with both families will help to establish a basic foundation on which the young couple can begin their married life. Parents can help the adjustment period for this young couple by being understanding and thoughtful.

Six Steps for Happy Mothers-in-law

(1) Be honest and be yourself—There is no need to put on any front or false pretense. Your own child will certainly see through it and will wonder what has happened to mother! If "being yourself" is not good enough, then you need to work on improving yourself when you are alone. The Bible says to speak the truth in love (Ephesians 4:15). If the truth is always spoken, then you will not need to be concerned with what you have said before; it will be loving truth. In fact, during the writing of

this book there have been times when I have had to speak the truth in love and tell my married children that I was unable to babysit. This did not cause resentment; they appreciated the truth.

(2) Be considerate of their rights and don't impose on them—Remember that they are a family unit now. The man is the head of his household; it is their home. They deserve the right of privacy, whether it be in their home or yours. Particularly if they are recently married, they deserve a time to adjust and acquaint themselves with married life. You may, in good faith, think you are helping by offering your services, but most young couples want to do things themselves. Be sensitive to their desires and do not impose yourself upon them.

(3) Be sure to treat both partners equally—Marriage unites a husband and wife as one, and that is the way you should respond to them. Letters, gifts, and remembrances should be equally distributed. One young wife told me that her mother-in-law always addressed her letters to her son. Such a mother stands the chance of separating her own child from her when she does not equally treat and accept the other partner. My daughter is blessed with a mother-in-law who is a talented seamstress and delights in sewing for her. My daughter wears these outfits proudly, and they represent to her that she is loved equally and accepted.

(4) Be careful not to criticize one partner to the other—Just good common sense tells you that this is unwise. One of the best ways to stop criticism is to reject it. Do not allow your son or daughter to criticize their partner to you. You should never negatively discuss one partner with the other. I overheard a mother-in-law

criticize her daughter-in-law to her son regarding an unwise purchase she had made. She was planting a seed of discontent in the son's mind. In doing so, she was also driving a wedge between herself and her son.

(5) Be careful not to mind their business or give unsolicited advice—You may not like the way they spend their money or their time but do not tell them so. If it is serious, then discuss it with your Heavenly Father and leave it there! By no means should you advise them on how to raise their children. You have had your day; now give this couple their chance to instill their principles for living in their own offspring. If you have done a good job, then sit back and let them put into practice what you have taught them. Advice should only be given when it is specifically asked for, and then very carefully.

(6) Be sure that your attitude is controlled by the Holy Spirit—Your attitude toward them should be accepting them as one, loving them in the Spirit, and leaving them in the hands of the Lord. In doing this you will succeed in being a gracious, godly mother-in-law.

The Contentment of Being a Grandmother

The grandmother who lives a Christ-controlled life will be a gentle, loving, and gracious person who is able to accept the role of being a grandparent. The traditional picture of a grandmother is one who is wise and can do no wrong. For some reason, little children look to their grandparents as being special creatures who know everything about everything. One mother told me that whenever she ran into something that she wasn't sure about, her child would say, "Let's ask Grandma; she will know." Grandmothers are expected to be saintly women with a special straight line to Heaven. Now that I have become a grandmother, I realize that that just isn't so. I didn't suddenly become a super-wise woman with a special spiritual endowment on the day my first grandchild was born. I am today what I have been becoming, the product of Him who controls my life.

It is true that a grandmother can have a great influence on a child's early years. Many a child has been led to Christ at his grandmother's knee. Because she is not usually involved in the work and upkeep of a child, she is able to spend time talking, reading, and playing with him. Her influence can be toward spiritual things or just plain fun. When the grandchildren are left in her care, the secure and mature grandmother will have no problem with disciplining and training the children rather than spoiling them by letting wrong-doings go unnoticed. There is one area where I feel wiser as a grandmother than I did as a mother; I believe I was often too rigid, whereas now I am more relaxed in some areas. There are some things that are absolute "no-no's" for the good of the child's welfare and for the sake of others around him. But some things that I used to feel very strongly about, I now tolerate; a child needs a certain amount of freedom, provided he is not harmed and the rights of others are not imposed upon. It is very important to respect the rules and guidelines that your son and daughter have laid down for their children. When they say, "No candy before dinner," then there should be no candy before dinner. The child needs to know that Grandma is in complete agreement with his parents. When the mother or father discipline the child, there is no need for Grandma to put in her "two-cents' worth"; instead, it is better for her to fade into the woodwork.

The way sons or daughters raise their own family is a real test of how well the parents have trained them and instilled into their hearts the basic principles for living. This should be a challenge to young parents to train their children properly while they have the opportunity. The day will come when they will see their children training their grandchildren either with or without many of the same values and principles.

The contented grandmother will have much to praise the Lord for! Her attitudes toward life and her children will be Christ-controlled. She may have the privilege of seeing her children reproduce and then her grandchildren reproduce. The joy will come when she sees them all in the family of God and knows that it was the love which she and her husband shared with one another that started it all. Her children will rise up and call her blessed.

> Her children rise up and call her blessed; her husband also, and he praiseth her.
>
> *Proverbs 31:28*

12

THE JOY OF HURTING

It was a dark day for me when the doctor diagnosed my increasing pain and discomfort as rheumatoid arthritis. At first the words meant little to me; then he went on to explain that this was a crippling disease. However, the full impact did not hit me until I was driving home on the freeway. Hot tears began to run down my cheeks and I wondered what the future held for me. I was going through ten days of testing diagnosis at a famous research clinic. Next day my appointment was with the physical therapist. It seemed like my world was caving in as I heard her say, "Here are the exercises you must do each day to retard the loss of motion you will no doubt experience." Some of the motion was already gone, and I knew what she said had much truth in it.

The next few days and weeks seemed to drag by. I did not feel well; the aching and hurting made matters seem worse. I began to question God, "Why me? You have just opened a new speaking ministry for me and now this!" Being the temperament I am, I tend to look on the darker side of circumstances. Since the hospital had fitted me for special shoes as well as braces for my hands, I knew I faced the same end result as the other patients I saw in that hospital—a wheel chair. I did a lot of crying in those days and drifted into periods of depression. Thank God for a husband who is optimistic and has great faith! After one particularly pessimistic experience, he announced to me that I was never again to visualize myself in a wheel chair. Instead, I was to look forward to the day when I would be completely whole. He said, "We have asked God to heal you; now let's expect Him to do it. From now on, picture yourself healed." I don't know if my husband really believed this or not, but he was so convincing to me that I accepted his words and began again to trust God. Things did begin to look brighter and my spirits improved.

My ministry continued and I promised the Lord that I would accept speaking engagements in spite of my pain and would depend on Him to supply the necessary strength and physical capability. There were many times when I boarded a plane in San Diego feeling only like going home to bed. But because of God's faithfulness, each time I reached my destination the pain and aching subsided enough to allow me to speak. In fact, the greater my personal pain the more liberty and power I seemed to have.

Life was going on at a reasonable pace and I seemed to be able to endure the pain and swelling of my joints by taking eighteen aspirin a day as recommended by my doctor. Some motion had been lost, but I seemed able to adjust to this even though the aspirin created a maddening ringing in my ears. The next blow came when I met a lovely lady who told me that she had been in far worse shape than I and God had instantly healed her. Again I questioned, "God, why not me? Have I not been faithful in my speaking ministry to women? Is there something more I must do? Do I have some unconfessed sin?" I prayed, I begged, I pleaded. I expected God to heal me! Yet in His marvelous wisdom He chose not to, and the pain increased. In fact, we took a trip to Europe and my feet hurt so badly I had a miserable time. Gradually a bitterness set in and I seemed to resent people who told me of others who had been healed. Very honestly, my spirit was not very attractive. I confessed this, and God removed all traces of bitterness from me long before He healed me.

Today I can thank God for dealing with me as He did. I have learned much about God's grace being sufficient for all our needs. God has given me a perfect peace.

> Thou wilt keep him in perfect peace, whose mind is stayed on thee, because he trusteth in thee.
>
> *Isaiah 26:3*

Since making my peace with God, He has taken away my pain and discomfort. Some would say that God put this disease into remission. I choose to believe that God had His own way of healing me, not instantly as some have testified, but over a long period of time so I could learn some very important life-changing lessons. My heart is overwhelmed with joy and gratitude today as I write out this manuscript word by word. Two years ago I was unable to close my hand around a pen long enough to write my name. But more than that, I thank God for the beautiful lessons He has taught me.

It was far more important for me to experience this abiding peace, to taste of the goodness of the Lord, to have my longing soul satisfied with His dear presence during my times of intense need than to have my physical body made whole. Through this I have learned that God does not deal with everyone in the same way but that He makes available to all His goodness and His mercy that endureth forever. He has filled my life with joy; surely my cup runneth over.

> Thou wilt show me the path of life. In thy presence is fullness of joy; at thy right hand there are pleasures forevermore.
>
> *Psalms 16:11*

Several years ago my husband and I were privileged to know a dear saint who was dying from cancer. She was the most radiant Christian lady we had ever known, a real saint with skin on. God did not heal her body, but she was so filled with the Spirit that we were never fully aware of the extent of her misery. In spite of the fact that she was bedridden and paralyzed, she was a blessing to everyone who visited her. We know of three people she led to Christ at her bedside, and only the Lord knows the scores of other people who had their lives changed because of her Christ-like influence.

> And he said unto me, My grace is sufficient for thee: for my strength is made perfect in weakness. Most gladly

therefore will I rather glory in my infirmities, that the power of Christ may rest upon me.

2 Cor. 12:9

13

TEMPERAMENT AND YOUR LOVE LIFE

The most powerful single influence on a person's behavior, humanly speaking, is his temperament. Although background, childhood training, education, environment, and a host of other factors make an impression on us, nothing is more significant than the temperament traits we inherit at birth, for they produce our actions, reactions, and motivations. Training can make a shy woman more outgoing, but she will never become a comfortable extrovert. Education will discipline the dynamic, aggressive individual, but it can never transform her into Mrs. Minnie Mouse. People are born either extroverts or introverts because these characteristics are an outgrowth of their temperament.

Since temperament has such an influence on a person's behavior, it follows that it will have a profound effect on another very powerful human instinct, the sex drive. In fact, a couple's intimate bedroom responses will often be a reflection of their temperament. Although most Christians seldom relate the Holy Spirit and married lovemaking, you will find a person's relationship with God will influence this intimate area of marriage. As my husband and I have shown in our book, *The Act of Marriage* (published by Zondervan Publishing House, Grand Rapids, Michigan, 1976), we are convinced that Christians properly motivated by the Spirit enjoy a better married love life than anyone else in today's society. Our detailed sex survey taken from 1700 Christian couples revealed that Christians not only scored themselves ten points higher in satisfaction in this area than non-Christians but that Spirit-filled Christians registered seven points higher than the non-Spirit-controlled.

Since lovemaking involves both the husband and the wife, let's examine each of the four temperaments in both sexes to demonstrate how they are most likely to respond sexually. We will first consider responses, appetites, hang-ups, and basic needs—then I will offer some suggestions for wives on how to become the kind of marriage partner for which God created them.

The Sanguine Husband

Sam Sanguine is so responsive that it doesn't take much to "turn him on," and since he is so obvious about everything he does, his wife is instantly aware of his mood. A natural charmer, he thinks he can turn the head of a female marble statue with his flattery. And he can—unless he is married to her. He usually has a great appetite for everything, including lovemaking.

Most sanguines have very few hang-ups about sex and usually make it clear they enjoy it. If it isn't the most important thing in life for them, it's a close second. The sanguine husband is usually reluctant to take "no" for an answer; in fact, he can easily be hurt or deflated if his partner does not respond to his gestures of love. He may outwardly project the idea that he is God's gift to women, but underneath he has a great need for affection. If he is not satisfied at home, Sam, more than any other temperament, may seek affection elsewhere for two reasons: (1) the conquest of another woman is necessary to satisfy his powerful ego, and he finds lonely, unfulfilled women easy prey to his charm; (2) he is weak-willed and emotionally excitable; consequently, he is vulnerable to the unscrupulous woman.

Sam Sanguine's needs—The supersex emphasis of our day is very hard on Sam, for he is easily stimulated. He has four basic needs in this area:

(1) Moral principles deeply ingrained in his heart and mind from childhood that show God's plan for one man for one woman "so long as they both shall live."

(2) The concept of "walking in the Spirit," particularly in his thought life. Romans 13:14 says, "Make no provision [forethought] for the flesh to fulfill it in the lusts thereof." If a sanguine indulges in immoral "fantasies," he will soon fan his passions out of control and will commit the sin of adultery to the heartache of his wife and himself. Once the moral barrier is broken, it is easy for him to repeat his sin.

(3) A loving, responsive, affectionate wife who freely

lets her husband know how much she enjoys his love. Husbands treated like that rarely stray, regardless of their temperament.

(4) A wife who becomes the *sole* object of his exuberant affection. He must avoid the flirtations and flattery of other women (thereby reassuring both his own wife and other women's husbands). Also, he should concentrate on bringing joy and fulfillment to his wife.

The Sanguine Wife

Very few differences in sexual response distinguish a sanguine man from a sanguine woman. Sarah Sanguine is a cheerful, happy, affectionate cheerleader type who has the gift of making men feel "comfortable" in her presence. Her charming personality makes her a "hit" with all types of men, and in her naivete she can turn them on without realizing it. She usually thinks she is "just being friendly."

As a wife, Sarah has a tremendous amount of love to impart to her husband and family. Lovemaking is very important to her, and it doesn't usually take too much coaxing to get her into the mood. Even if hurt or angry, she rather easily can moderate her attitude. Sanguines rarely carry a grudge, a trait essential for any marriage! She is the most likely type to greet her husband at the door with a "kiss with a future." Of all the temperaments, she is the one most likely to jolt her husband, after reading *The Total Woman*, by meeting him at the door dressed in boots and an apron. Since she rarely has hang-ups about anything, she usually maintains a good attitude toward sex, often in spite of disastrously distorted misconceptions handed down from her mother. Her natural ability to express herself overcomes her inhibitions, and she quickly finds that she heightens her lovemaking enjoyment by being aggressive. Unless unwisely stifled by her husband, she usually learns early that passivity in lovemaking is not for her. Her sanguine mood-swings vary, bringing great delight to her partner. These wives have a tremendous desire to please their partners. With a reasonable amount of encouragement and cooperation, they usually succeed in this area of marriage, provided their shortcomings in other areas do not become their partner's obsessions.

Sarah Sanguine's needs—The fun-loving Sarah Sanguines start out in marriage expecting to enjoy it. The following suggestions will help them to realize that potential:

(1) Cultivate a strong spiritual life by walking in the Spirit, regularly studying the Word of God, and obeying His standards of moral behavior.

(2) Recognize her ability to excite men other than her husband and avoid flirtations that would provoke his jealousy or confront her with temptations.

(3) Soften her extroversion so she will not embarrass her husband. It is especially important to learn that a loud, overbubbly wife may gain the attention of other men but disapproval from her husband.

(4) Dearly love a mate who will assure her of this approval and acceptance and dispense tender words of encouragement, attention, and affection. If she receives these, she will give attention to proper grooming, fashion, manners, good housekeeping, and whatever else will make her pleasing to her husband.

The Choleric Husband

On the surface a choleric suitor appears to be a great

lover. Candy and flowers in abundance, politeness, kindness, and dynamic leadership make him appear to be the embodiment of manliness. Somehow that tends to change shortly after marriage. Cholerics are such goal-conscious creatures that they are willing to do almost anything to attain their desires. Since the "sweet young thing" is subconsciously a goal before marriage, the choleric is willing to pay any price to win her hand. Once married, however, the goal is changed—now he wants to support her properly. Consequently, he may work from twelve to twenty hours a day. The hardest thing for a choleric male to understand is that his partner did not marry him for what he could give her but for himself. When confronted with his wife's complaint that he doesn't love her anymore, he responds, "Of course I love you; I work like a slave to give you what you want." The truth of the matter is, he enjoys work.

Emotionally, a choleric is an extremist; he is either hot or cold. He can get furiously angry and explode over trifles, and his bride becomes terrified when she first sees these outbursts. His impatience and inability to lavish affection on her may produce a difficult adjustment for her. Showing affection is just "not his thing." One woman married to a choleric said, "Kissing my husband is like kissing a marble statue in the cemetery on a winter day."

The choleric's impetuous traits likewise hinder his proper adjustment to marriage. Just as he is apt to set out on a trip before consulting a road map, he is prone to take his wife to the bedroom without the slightest sex education. Somehow he thinks it will all work out!

Fortunely, a choleric possesses one important trait

that helps his love life: he is always practical. Once he realizes that lovemaking involves more than preparing for a 100-yard dash—that he must be tender, gentle, affectionate, thoughtful, and sensitive to his wife's needs—he learns quickly. In the learning process he finds that affection is exciting and that watching the woman he loves respond to his touch is extremely fulfilling.

Carl Choleric's needs—The most underdeveloped part of a choleric is his emotional life. And since lovemaking at its best is motivated by emotion, he has many needs:

(1) To show love and compassion for others. Nothing short of the personal experience of receiving Christ as Lord and Savior and learning to "walk in the Spirit" will provide the choleric with this ability. Even after his conversion it often takes some time before the "love of God" characterizes his life.

(2) To understand that many people are not as self-sufficient as he. Even though they may be as capable, they will not be as confident that they can perform well. Carl must realize that other people may tend to harbor doubts much more easily than he. If he will patiently show kindness and encourage his partner, she will be a better performer.

(3) To develop tenderness and affection for his wife and children and to voice his approval and commendation of them. He must learn to address an "I love you" quite frequently to his wife and act proud of her. Because the choleric is a natural leader, others tend to look to him for approval, love, and acceptance. He can wither them with a disapproving look and condemning word, or he can lift their spirits by going out of his way to approve

and commend them. Those who have been rejected by him may tend to build a shell around their egos in order to protect themselves and to ward off future injuries. When the choleric father and husband becomes sensitive to the emotional needs of his family, he can even spark emotions within himself that would otherwise remain dormant. To say "I love you" is not easy, but when he forgets himself, recognizing the importance of these words to his loved one and concentrating on her emotional well-being, Carl will learn quickly—and he will thoroughly enjoy the response it brings.

(4) To eliminate sarcasm and disrespectful speech from his vocabulary. Unkind and resentful words never turn a wife on!

(5) To learn to overcome his inner hostilities and anger for two reasons: first, "grieving the Spirit" through anger (Ephesians 4:30-32) will keep him a spiritual pygmy all of his Christian life; second, the threat of instant choleric explosion inhibits the emotional expressions of his wife. It is difficult for a choleric Christian to realize that his spiritual life will affect his bedroom life, but it does—one way or the other.

The Choleric Wife

Clara Choleric is usually an exciting creature, particularly if one does not have to live with her. She is extremely active in every area of life—a dynamic, forceful individual with multiple goals in mind. At the same time she may feature a spitfire personality and a razor-blade tongue, dominating and controlling every activity in which she is involved.

In my late teens there was such a girl in our youth

group. Many guys dated her because she was fun to be with, but they kiddingly remarked behind her back, "Don't marry Evelyn unless you want to be president of the United States."

The necessity of having a positive mental attitude toward lovemaking in marriage comes into focus when dealing with the choleric wife. If she observed a warm love relationship between her parents while she was growing up, she will probably enter marriage expecting to enjoy lovemaking. Cholerics usually achieve what they set out to do, and she will probably not be disappointed—nor will her husband.

On the other hand, if she has been raised by unhappy, bickering parents, if she has been molested or has endured other traumatic experiences in childhood, or if she has been taught that "sex is dirty" for either religious or other ill-conceived reasons, she may encounter serious difficulty in relating properly to her husband. Cholerics are so opinionated that once obsessed with the idea that "sex is not for nice girls," they might reject the angel Gabriel carrying a message on a stone tablet saying "marriage is honorable in all." But once convinced that God wants her to enjoy sex, she can usually make a quick transition to a happy love life.

Choleric wives often acquire several potential hangups in this department. They are not usually given to open affection, and thus they often stifle their husbands' advances before their own motor rolls into action. In addition, if not Spirit-filled, they tend to demasculinize a man by dominating and leading him in everything— including sex. It takes a Spirit-led, thoughtful choleric woman to recognize that she ignores her husband's ego at her own peril.

We have observed that opposites attract each other in marriage; consequently, a choleric woman will usually select a passive partner. If she isn't especially fond of lovemaking, they may go for long periods without it because he may be too passive to say or do anything about it. Whether or not he raises the issue, you can be sure he doesn't enjoy the abstinence! Ultimately an explosion occurs—and almost always with serious consequences.

It is to the choleric wife's credit, however, that she will usually adjust and become a very enjoyable partner once she learns how important a good bedroom life is to her husband. She must realize that the success of her marriage may well depend upon her performance and willingness to let her husband maintain leadership in this intimate area of their life.

Clara Choleric's needs—Like her male counterpart, Clara Choleric has many needs. These are some of the most important for her to consider:

(1) To "walk in the Spirit" in order to provide victory over her hot temper and sarcastic tongue and to develop her emotional capability in showing love and affection. Being loving and affectionate is certainly easier for some temperaments than others, but God would never have commanded that we love one another if He had not known it was possible for all. Cholerics may need to work at it a little harder than some, but the more they express it, the easier it comes.

(2) To learn forgiveness—especially for her father, if necessary. No woman can fully enjoy her husband if she hates her father. This is especially true of strong-minded, opinionated, willful cholerics. They will vent their frus-

trated wrath on their husbands, stifling their expressions of love. One reason a choleric woman may have this problem is that as a little girl she may have resisted her father's affections, and because he did not understand, he closed her out of his heart and had little to do with her—he simply did not know how to reach her. Not realizing why she was rejected by her daddy, she increasingly withdrew from showing any normal expressions of emotion toward him and fostered a growing resentment toward men.

(3) To avoid heaping sarcasm, criticism, and ridicule on her husband, particularly in the lovemaking area. Cholerics exude so much self-confidence that, even without saying anything, they cause others to feel inadequate. The choleric woman needs to let her husband know how much she values him as a man and a lover. No compliment is sweeter and cherished longer than one which appreciates the masculinity or femininity of one's partner.

(4) To take time to express love to her husband. Cholerics are often night people. Early-bird husbands may crawl into bed at ten or eleven o'clock, hoping for a little tenderness and love, but they fall asleep while their choleric wives finish a book, clean the house, or pursue countless other activities which their active minds suggest. Many choleric wives could improve their love lives just by going to bed earlier.

(5) To learn submission by Biblical standards. A choleric likes to lead and usually makes a good leader, but by the grace of God and in obedience to His Word, such a wife needs to bring herself into submission to her husband. If she attempts to assume the husband's role and

responsibilities in the home, she is courting disaster. A passive husband will give his wife more love, respect, and flexibility if she encourages him to take the responsibility and leadership of their home.

The Melancholic Husband

Marvin Melancholy is a supreme idealist. He usually goes into marriage without any sex education because he idealistically believes that everything will work out. If he is blessed with an amorous and exciting wife who has no hang-ups, everything usually does work out, but if he marries someone as naive as he, they may come home from their honeymoon in a depressed state. When the love life of a couple is deficient, it can create a shaky experience for a melancholic husband. His wife will especially be turned off by his depression, further complicating matters. It is usually quite difficult for him to seek counseling until his marriage enters a precarious phase.

The melancholic, more than any other temperament, has the capacity to express true love. He is a loyal and faithful partner unless he overindulges in impure thoughts and becomes involved in promiscuity. When Marvin Melancholy loves his wife, he will almost overextend himself in thoughtfulness, kindness, and emotion.

Among the melancholic's greatest assets is his romanticism, so he does the work of preparation beautifully: soft music, dim lights, perfume—those things that delight the romantic heart of a woman.

Because he is extremely analytical, Martin quickly learns what his wife finds pleasurable and enjoys bringing her to fulfillment. If everything goes well for them, this couple can become great lovers.

Unfortunately, everything in life doesn't always turn out perfectly, and marriage is no exception. Melancholics are such perfectionists that they almost refuse to accept anything less than perfection. Many a melancholic man can come home all "revved up" for his wife only to have his ardor cooled by dirty dishes in the sink or kids' toys in the middle of the floor. In fact, I know one melancholic husband who could be turned on by watching his wife get undressed for bed and turned off because she didn't hang up her clothes. At a time like that, a sanguine or choleric wouldn't even notice the clothes!

The sensitive traits of the melancholic that on most occasions make him aware of his wife's needs for tenderness and love may also work against him at times. He is prone to interpret his wife's lack of immediate response when he first initiates lovemaking as rejection. If his wife is in a coy mood, as women frequently are, and wants mild pursuit, he is apt to think she doesn't desire him and gives up before she can reveal her true feelings.

Marvin Melancholy needs—The melancholic individual has a tremendous amount of love to give to others if granted the slightest encouragement. These are some of his most obvious needs:

(1) Maintaining a vital, personal relationship with God and a daily Spirit-filled experience that keeps him "other-oriented" instead of obsessed with himself. No selfish or self-centered person will be a good lover, no matter what his temperament. A real test of whether or not a melancholic is walking in the Spirit appears when he breaks that self-centered syndrome.

(2) Learning to give unconditional love, not rewarded love. A wife once told me that her husband was a

natural-born nit-picker. "He has a long check-list for housekeeping, and if I don't rate an 'A' before we go to bed, he will not make love to me," she complained.

(3) Avoiding a critical and pessimistic attitude, the two biggest problems of a melancholic. Because of his perfectionism, he often expects unrealistic standards of achievement for himself and others. This in turn causes him to become frequently disillusioned when things and people don't measure up.

(4) Maintaining a positive and wholesome thought life (Philippians 4:8). He should never indulge in revengeful thought patterns or self-pity, but always "give thanks in everything" (1 Thessalonians 5:18).

(5) Being married to a woman who is not easily offended and can cheerfully encourage him when he is down, reassure him of his manhood when he is insecure, and take his criticism lightly. As long as she knows he is moody, she can patiently wait a little while for his mood to change.

(6) Concentrating on God and thanking Him for his partner's strengths. He must regularly encourage her with verbal assurances of love and approval. I have seen many a sanguine wife go through a personality change under the constant criticism of a melancholic husband. Unfortunately, when he is finished even Marvin Melancholy doesn't like his creation.

The Melancholic Wife

Martha Melancholy is an unpredictable love partner, for she has the greatest of all mood swings. On some occasions she can be as exciting and stimulating as any sanguine. On others she has absolutely no interest in anything—including love. She may meet her husband at the door and sweep him off his feet right into the bedroom, or she may ignore his arrival completely.

Martha Melancholy is the supreme romantic, and her moods are as apparent as the noonday sun. When in the mood for love, she resorts to dinner by candlelight, soft music, and heavy perfume. (If she's married to a sanguine, that works quite well; but if her husband is a choleric, she may be in trouble, because he often detests perfume.)

Although she has the capability of enjoying ecstatic love at heights that would asphyxiate other temperaments, she rarely is interested in setting world records for frequency. To her, quality is always preferable to quantity. Of all the temperament types, she is the most apt to engage in bedroom roulette—that is, she dispenses love as a reward for good behavior. However, no man worthy of the title will put up with that!

A melancholic is often plagued with unreal prudishness, especially if her mother had a problem in this area. She may use trumped-up religious arguments to excuse her sexual abstinence; her real problem, however, probably stems from her premarital resolution that sex is undesirable, and she has never given herself the opportunity to learn otherwise. She is the type that saves lovemaking only for propagation—never for pleasure. A study of the Scriptures can teach her differently.

Little things can quickly be turned into mountainous problems for Martha Melancholy. Her husband's inability to balance the check book, his forgetting to run an errand, or his neglect to bathe may thoroughly upset her and send her into quiet revenge. She feels he didn't keep his part of a bargain, so she need not keep hers—and thus she refrains from lovemaking. What she doesn't realize is that she is cheating herself out of both the enjoyment of lovemaking and the loving approval of her husband.

I counseled a melancholic wife who had not made love with her partner for several weeks. She was only interested at night, but by the time she was ready for bed, he had collapsed. She complained, "He goes to bed tired, and he never even takes time to bathe or brush his teeth. In the morning I am a zombie and he is charged up. But I can't stand his body smells and bad breath then!" I suggested that she learn to accept her husband and not try to change him. This was hard medicine for a wife to take, but before long she discovered that by cooperating with him, he was quite willing to modify his habits for her.

Another hang-up common to Martha Melancholy is jealousy. Not given to "insincere flirtation," she often marries a man who is outgoing and friendly to all. It is not uncommon for her to ride home in icy silence after a party because her husband "flirted with every woman there." Since her husband's male ego gets so little food at home, he unwisely seeks it at social gatherings. And he may often think, "Nothing I do ever satisfies that woman!"

Seated across from the beautiful wife of a wealthy and dynamic Christian businessman, I was startled to hear his melancholic wife ask me, "Would you explain why I am so jealous of my husband even when I know I have no reason for it?" It seems that he had dismissed three successive secretaries and finally hired the homeliest gal he could find just because of his wife's jealousy, but it still didn't solve her problem. I responded, "The problem is not with your husband; you just don't like yourself." Tears ran down her cheeks as she admitted to strong feelings of self-rejection. Later, her husband commented concerning their love life, "When her groundless suspicions make her jealous, I can't touch her. But when she is sorry for her accusations, she can't get enough of me. I never know whether to expect feast or famine!"

Martha's biggest problem in life will be the tendency toward self-pity. A melancholic can follow the slightest insult or rejection with self-pitying thoughts that plunge her into a state of depression until she is not interested in love or anything else.

Martha Melancholy's needs—The emotional capability of a melancholic is so extensive that she has the potential of being an exciting and fulfilling love partner if her weaknesses don't overpower her strengths. Here are some of her specific needs:

(1) A vital and effective relationship with Jesus Christ, walking in His Spirit, so that she may enjoy the love, peace, and joy He gives to make her an effective person.

(2) A thankful attitude for all the blessings God has given her, never thinking or verbalizing criticism for the things that don't please her. She will discover that a positive mental attitude combined with thanksgiving can give her a happier outlook on life and make her a more pleasant person for others to enjoy. This attitude will also help her to accept herself as she is; self-condemnation will destroy her. It is very difficult for others to like her if she does not like herself.

(3) Acceptance of her husband as he is, permitting God to make any changes that are needed. Her submis-

sion to him should not be dependent on his behavior but on her obedience to God.

(4) Encouragement and reassurances of love from her husband. A thoughtful and verbally expressive husband who proves his love in many other areas of their marriage will be rewarded in this one.

(5) The request that God give her an unconditional love for her husband and the ability to love him to the point that she forgets about herself. She needs to realize that married love is beautiful because it is God's plan for married partners. Our Lord promises that a woman who gives herself without reservations to her husband will be loved. He said, "Give and it shall be given unto you," and "Whatsoever a man soweth, that shall he also reap." If a woman sows love, she will surely reap it in abundance.

(6) The lesson of forgiveness. Almost every durable marriage requires forgiveness along the way. Because an unforgiving attitude will always destroy a relationship, the partners must realize that their harmony requires it and God commands it (Matthew 18:35; Mark 11:25).

The Phlegmatic Husband

Not much is known about the bedroom life of Philip Phlegmatic. He is without doubt the world's most closed-mouth individual, particularly concerning his personal life. What is known about this intimate area usually comes from an irate partner; consequently, the information could well be biased. In fairness to the phlegmatic male, therefore, any suggestions we make concerning his lovemaking responses have to be evaluated on the basis of deductive analysis and hearsay reporting.

Some assume that because a phlegmatic is easy-going and prone to be unmotivated, he may not be a very spirited lover, but that may not always be true. If a study of the habits of phlegmatics is indicative, we find that they usually accomplish more than they are given credit for. They just don't make noise and attract much attention to their achievements like other temperaments. Rather, they make good use of the effort expended. When they want to do something, they follow through effectively and promptly in their own quiet way. We suspect that is the way they make love.

One characteristic of phlegmatics should help their love life: their abundant kindness. Rarely, if ever, would Philip Phlegmatic embarrass or insult his wife; sarcasm is just not his way. Women usually respond to a man who is kind to them. On that basis he should have little trouble gaining love from his wife.

Another trait that is surely a great advantage is that a phlegmatic rarely gets angry and seldom creates irritation in others. If his fiery partner screams at him for some reason, his response usually extinguishes the fire because he is a master of the "soft answer." Consequently, the storm has usually passed by bedtime, and he can conveniently act as if it never happened.

Phlegmatic men often have a way of getting things to go their way by waiting for them. They are patience personified, apparently able to outwait others into action. Their love life is probably like that. As the intensity of their youthful sex drive cools down somewhat, they patiently teach their partner to originate lovemaking. If the truth were known, they probably get all the love they want in marriage, perhaps more frequently and better than some of the more tempestuous types. They are simply more prone than other temperaments to let their partner initiate lovemaking.

Three areas may cause the phlegmatic man serious trouble. First, he tends to be reluctant to assert himself and take leadership unless it is thrust upon him. When he does lead, he performs his tasks admirably. However, when he fails to take the leadership in the home, his wife can become very disillusioned. The wife who expects such a husband to assume the initiative in the bedroom may soon feel unloved. Sometimes she loses respect for her phlegmatic husband because he doesn't seem to assert his manhood.

A second danger spot is phlegmatic selfishness, making him stingy, stubborn (in a polite way), and self-indulgent. Yielding to these weaknesses can produce resentment in a wife who complains, "He doesn't give me enough grocery money, and he never takes me out. All we ever do is what he wants to do." As we have already seen, resentment stifles love.

The third potential danger area to a phlegmatic is that he tends to crawl into a shell of silence when things fail to work out. Since he usually finds it difficult to talk about anything, he probably finds it hard to teach his partner what he finds exciting in lovemaking. Consequently, he will silently endure subpar relations for years and cheat both himself and his partner out of countless ecstatic experiences which God meant them to enjoy.

Philip Phlegmatic's needs—The kindhearted, soft-spoken, gentle phlegmatic may appear to outsiders as a man who has conquered his weaknesses, but those who live with him recognize his salient needs. These are some of the most pertinent:

(1) A dynamic relationship to Jesus Christ that motivates him to think of the needs of his wife and family rather than indulge in his own feelings and solitude.

(2) A more aggressive attitude in everything, especially in consideration of his wife's needs in lovemaking.

(3) Greater expression of his love and approval for his wife. He must learn to talk more freely about his own desires and needs, especially if the couple is confronting problems. This need to communicate requires his continual efforts.

(4) A wife who will understand and accept his seeming lack of motivation without resentment, one who will tactfully use her feminine wiles in arousing him at the appropriate time.

(5) A wife who will try to adapt her metabolic timetable to her partner's to maximize what vitality he has, one who appreciates his strong, silent tendencies and recognizes the depth of his nature, giving thanks for it rather than chafing at his inclination toward passivity. If she starts nagging, he will crawl into his shell and shut her out.

The Phlegmatic Wife

As a general rule, the easiest person in the world to get along with is a phlegmatic, especially a woman. She loves to please people and usually gives in to her more forceful mate rather than create turmoil. She is easily satisfied and often turns her affection and attention on her children if trouble arises between her and her husband.

Her passive personality will usually characterize her

bedroom life; she rarely initiates lovemaking, but because she wants to please her partner, she almost never turns him down.

One of the most powerful influences in a phlegmatic's life, an influence which will strongly affect her lovemaking, may be fear and the anxiety which it causes. Such a woman may fear pregnancy (although she doesn't have a corner on that problem), disclosure, embarrassment, and a host of other real and imagined dilemmas. One of her biggest fears is that her husband may lose respect for her if she appears eager or forward in lovemaking, though quite the opposite is the usual reaction.

Polly Phlegmatic's needs—In spite of her gracious, kind, and pleasant spirit, she has several needs to become a better wife and love partner:

(1) To accept Jesus Christ as her Lord and Savior. Many phlegmatics have a hard time acknowledging that they are sinners (and they act so nice that others will likely agree, but self-righteousness has kept many out of the Kingdom of God). As she learns to "walk in the Spirit" each day, the phlegmatic woman will gain motivation to overcome her passivity, love to overcome her selfishness, and faith to overcome her fears. When armed with such attributes from God, she can become an exciting partner.

(2) To create and maintain an interest in her appearance. Phlegmatic mothers often get so tired after their babies arrive that they become careless about their personal appearance—their hair, their attire, and often their weight. When a wife ceases to care how she looks to her man, she has clearly lost her self-esteem. Her husband's love and respect will also fade. A wife need not be a

raving beauty to maintain the high regard of her husband, but her appearance night after night will indicate what she thinks of herself and of her husband. Any man should appreciate the fact that his wife is tired once in awhile, but five nights a week is a cop-out.

Some Christian women have used 1 Peter 3:3 as an excuse to let their "outward appearance" run down—at the expense of their marriage. However, that passage really says that a godly wife will spend more time cultivating her spiritual life than her physical, but by no means does it teach that she is to neglect either one. Remember, a woman is the most beautiful flower in a man's garden, and even roses need to be cultivated, pruned, and cared for.

(3) To organize her daily life and sustain a regular schedule. A phlegmatic wife finds it easier to neglect her housekeeping chores than anyone else except a sanguine. She enjoys "koffee klatches"—and before she realizes it, hubby is due home. Since opposites attract each other, it is not uncommon for a phlegmatic wife to create such resentment in her more fastidious partner that it spills over into their bedroom life. His uncharitable outburst may cause a stubborn phlegmatic to "refuse to clean up," producing further disharmony. Consequently, she needs to take pride in homemaking; her husband will respect and treat her better, and even more importantly, she will respect herself more.

(4) To appreciate a thoughtful lover and strong, gentle husband. She requires a lover who learns how a woman functions best and takes time to arouse her to orgasm. Once she has learned that art, her desire for the experience will overpower her tendency to passivity, and she

can learn to be an exciting partner. He needs to be a strong, gentle husband from whom she can draw courage to overcome her fears, one who will encourage not browbeat her. A wise husband will verbally assure his wife of her worth and his love.

(5) To learn to overcome her inability to speak the words she feels and communicate with her husband and family. Words do not naturally come easily for her, especially about the intimacies of her love life. Phlegmatics need to push themselves in every area of life, and love-making is no exception! Polly Phlegmatic needs to remember the needs of her partner and forget her own; they will both be happier for it!

Conclusion

All four temperaments possess the capacity to become loving, satisfying marriage partners. As we have seen, each has its areas of strength and weakness. Consequently, each is capable of overcompensating in an area of strength or developing a hang-up in an area of weakness. For that reason, it is helpful for every partner to know her loved one's temperament so that she can approach him in the most suitable fashion. Remember— love gives! When a woman administers love, she will in return receive all the love she needs.

One of the advantages of knowing the four temperaments is that it becomes easier to appreciate why your partner acts or reacts the way he does. That in turn helps you to accept his individual foibles and work with them, not against them.

We have a lovely sanguine friend named Molly who told me how God used the temperaments to resolve a pet peeve that was hindering her love life. Her husband,

Pete, a melancholic-phlegmatic, regularly checked up on her. When he put his arm around her in bed as she snuggled close to him and warmed up to his mood, he would ask, "Molly, did you lock the back door and turn the heat down?" Though she answered, "Yes, Pete," he would jump out of bed, run through the dining room and kitchen and check the back door and the thermostat. By the time he returned, her mood had turned to ice and she gave him the cold shoulder. This went on night after night—except when he became amorous enough to forget to ask that aggravating question.

One night Pete, an accountant by profession, brought home several income tax reports, spread them out on the dining room table, and began to work. Molly stood in the doorway, watching a strange charade: four times he added up a column of figures, put the answer on a slip of paper, and turned it over. When he finished the fourth one, he turned them all right side up and smiled to himself—they all agreed, so he wrote the answer on the tax form. Suddenly Molly realized that Pete didn't just check up on her; he even double-checked himself! She was proud of his reputation as an accurate accountant, and now she realized that the striving for perfection which made him successful in business was the same trait that caused him to check up on her.

That night she was ready for him! He put his arm around her, and she snuggled up close as usual. But when he asked, "Molly, did you lock the back door, and what about the heat?" she sweetly replied, "I sure did, honey, but if you want to check, it's okay by me." He got up and trotted through the dining room and kitchen; as usual, the door was locked and the thermostat turned down. But that night when he crawled back into bed, he didn't encounter a frosty iceberg!

Once you have diagnosed your husband's temperament, you can lovingly cooperate with it instead of clash with him.

14

DIVORCE OR DEATH

One of the most traumatic experiences a woman can have in her lifetime is the death of her partner; next to that is divorce. In my husband's book, *How To Win Over Depression* (Zondervan Publishing House, Grand Rapids, 1974), he tells of a crisis scale developed by Dr. Thomas Holmes, professor of psychiatry at the University of Washington School of Medicine in Seattle. This system shows how much emotional stress each crisis in life creates. In a list of 43 events, the death of a spouse rated highest with a score of 100 points; divorce was listed second with a score of 73. More important than the intensity of the crisis is the mental attitude with which it is approached. When these events in a woman's life are faced with the courage and hope that the Heavenly Father provides, she will have victory over the problems of life.

I have cried, prayed, and empathized with individuals who have gone through these experiences. In preparation for the writing of this chapter, I have read every book and magazine article on the subject that I could lay my hands on. I have found that there is hope for the woman who is willing to take her eyes off herself and look to the Lord Jesus for help and strength.

> God is our refuge and strength, a very present help in trouble.
>
> *Psalms 46:1*

Widowed and divorced women probably have more ups and downs than any other group—a roller coaster existence—but God has provided a way for them to maintain order in their lives. He will be a stabilizing influence. It takes a moment-by-moment and day-by-day renewing of the inner man, a daily communing with the Heavenly Father.

> These sufferings of ours are for your benefit. And the more of you who are won to Christ, the more there are to thank Him for His great kindness, and the more the Lord is glorified. That is why we never give up. Though our bodies are dying, our inner strength in the Lord is growing every day. These troubles and sufferings of ours are, after all, quite small and won't last very long. Yet this short time of distress will result in God's richest blessing upon us forever and ever! So we do not look at what we can see right now, the troubles all around us, but we look forward to the joys of heaven which we have not yet seen. The troubles will soon be over, but the joys to come will last forever.
>
> *2 Corinthians 4:15-18*

Victory Over the Hurt of Divorce

If you are divorced, you certainly are not alone. Recently a marriage center disclosed these latest statistics on divorce:

Among 30-year-old wives, 1 out of every 3 marriages has been or will be dissolved in divorce.

In 21% of all marriages either one or both of the partners have been divorced.

1 child in 6 will lose a parent to divorce by the time he is 18 years old.

In 1975, for the first time in American history, we exceeded one million divorces.

These statistics could be multiplied, but there is no need since most people are fully aware of these increased tragedies in today's society. What we need to know is how to cope with the problems that stem from divorce.

During the stormy days that precede the divorce court there will be emotions of anger and bitterness—anger because you feel that someone has done you wrong and taken advantage of you and bitterness because you resent the circumstance in which you find yourself and are unable to make them come out the way you want them. These can only be remedied by asking the Lord's help in giving you a forgiving spirit. You must follow the instructions given in Ephesians 4:30-32 to "grieve not the Holy Spirit." All bitterness and anger are to be put away; we are told to be kind to one another, forgiving one another, even as God has forgiven us. If God is willing and able to forgive both partners, then surely we, too, can forgive!

A feeling of rejection and guilt usually follows the period of anger and bitterness. You feel rejected because someone you once loved, even enough to go to the marriage altar, has now hurt and rejected you either for someone else or for a life alone. You may feel guilty because you did not do things differently while there was still a chance or because you were not willing to give it another try. Once again, as long as you look at your shortcomings and what you might have done, there will be no victory in your life. It is only when you confess all this to Christ, thank Him for helping you through past difficulties, and trust Him for the future, that you will experience mental peace and be able to live the abundant life.

When you feel that life has not dealt fairly with you, you begin to pity yourself for all the hardships you have had to live through just because a man let you down. Your children may be suffering from the separation of their parents, and you again feel sorry for yourself that you could not provide them with a more normal and secure home life. Self-pity always causes depression. Your children will suffer not only because their home life has been disrupted but also because their mother is depressed and unable to give her very best to them. At a time like this children need at least one parent who is not distraught and can therefore share with them a life of stability and love. A mother needs to realize that she has the full responsibility for molding her children's emotional and spiritual lives. She should therefore look beyond herself to the needs of her family.

Some time ago a young woman told me the following story. Her husband had divorced her for another woman, and she was left to raise their two children by herself. He moved out of the state and did not see the children for months at a time. On one occasion, when he was traveling through their city, he called to ask if he could drop by and visit the children. She went the extra mile and even prepared dinner for him so he could see them a while longer. During the evening she noticed him glancing rather uneasily at a plaque on the wall. The plaque read, "Honor thy father and thy mother." The more he looked at the plaque, the more uneasy he became. Finally he said to her, "I suppose the kids hate me." She quickly answered, "On the contrary, they pray for you every night before they go to bed and they thank God for their daddy. I have never told them about any of our problems. They just wonder why they don't see their father very often." This wise mother had decided early in her divorce that more important than her problems was her children's need for as normal a life as she could possibly give them. She found that in giving to them she developed a contentment and a peace of mind. That little family had experienced the healing which results from a mother's unselfish heart and thanksgiving spirit.

To overcome feelings of self-pity and depression, the divorced woman needs to learn to have a thankful heart.

> In everything give thanks: for this is the will of God in Christ Jesus concerning you.
>
> *2 Thess. 5:18*

There is absolutely no way she can be depressed and have a thanksgiving heart. Many things will have to be accepted by faith, but she is instructed to give thanks in everything!

Then there is the terrible feeling of loneliness that sets in following the judge's final decree—"Divorce granted!" The wife who have been overly dependent upon her husband will now feel terribly alone in his absence. I have noted women who have panicked over their inability to cope with things as trivial as an upset glass of milk or a dog barking. In many cases, her sense of worth was so centered around her husband that without him she has lost her desire to live. One woman I know turned to drugs and alcohol after her husband walked out on her. She felt she had been a total failure and was not able to face reality. She attempted suicide and even failed at that; her self-image was so poor that it almost destroyed her. The woman who has enough self-esteem will be able to pull herself out of the loneliness and engage in activities that make her feel worthwhile and give her a purpose for living.

How does a woman gain a better self-image? First of all, you must follow the instructions given in Romans 12:3 "to think soberly of ourselves" as God has dealt a measure of faith to each of us. Evaluate yourself according to what God has done for you. If we have Christ living within us, then we have a basis for liking ourselves. It is "not I, but Christ" living in me that makes me a worthwhile being. Accept yourself as a special creation from the hand of God and thank Him for what He is going to do with your life in the future.

There will be times of disappointment when friends do not step forth to help you. There may be some unhappily married people who will look at you and think you really have it made—you are independent and free. On the other hand, there may be some who think "you got what you really deserved." Unfortunately, some people are more prone to criticize and condemn than ready to help. It hurts to be condemned and may cause you to feel guilty. Remember, God has forgiven you. Can you forgive yourself? Jesus said to the woman caught in the act of adultery, "Neither do I condemn thee; go, and sin no more." If you have confessed your sin, then God has forgiven you. If God Almighty forgives you, then certainly you should forgive yourself and not suffer from feelings of guilt and condemnation.

Unfortunately, women in this situation tend to set up temporary living habits. This is detrimental to both the woman and her children and will produce poor mental attitudes. It is far better to face the naked reality head-on than to just mark time. Take inventory of yourself; look closely to see what you can change, and then ask God to help you accept those things that are unchangeable.

We all have lessons to learn, and we all must learn these lessons in different ways. For some the pathway to learning seems much more difficult than it does for others. The important thing is to learn the lesson! You can be a great source of help and comfort to others if you have learned well. Around you are scores of women going through the same trauma and distress that you have experienced. You have a great ministry open to you if you have learned well and have allowed the Holy Spirit to comfort you and to control your life.

> Who comforteth us in all our tribulation, that we may be able to comfort them who are in any trouble by the comfort with which we ourselves are comforted of God. For as the sufferings of Christ abound in us, so our consolation also aboundeth by Christ.
>
> *2 Corinthians 1:4, 5*

Is God able or is He not? Is He able to help you over the loneliness of a Christmas Eve? Is He capable of helping you raise your fatherless children? Can God help to control your sexual desires? Will He provide the necessary strength to withstand temptation? Is He able to protect you from the dangers of living alone? These questions could go on endlessly. If God is able to succeed in one, He can succeed in all.

> But my God shall supply ALL your need according to his riches in glory by Christ Jesus.
>
> *Philippians 4:19*

Till Death Do Us Part

The widow faces many of the same emotional upsets as the divorcee—loneliness, self-pity, fear, depression. In addition, the loss of a husband produces grief and sorrow. In many cases, the woman has had to sit at the bedside of her dying husband and watch him die before her very eyes. Nobody knows why a dearly loved husband is taken except that it was God's plan for him. It is beyond our knowledge and we must trust the Heavenly Father for the future.

The widow receives help and sympathy for herself and her family because most people feel she was dealt an unfair blow. She does not have to face rejection and guilt as does the divorcee. However, if she continues to dwell on herself and her problems, she will in time develop a self-pitying "woe is me" attitude.

Great caution should be taken when the formerly married woman begins to date; this is true for both widows and divorcees. Many times men feel a little more free and loose around a woman who has been married. Because she is no longer a virgin, they tend to think she does not have to make as great a sacrifice to engage in intimate relations. Also, they sometimes feel that since she has had sex and perhaps developed an appetite for it, they are helping her out by getting her physically involved.

The widowed or divorced woman does not have to sacrifice her moral convictions in order to have companionship or to remarry. God honors those who have the courage to stand firm and not slacken their convictions. Do not sacrifice the permanent on the altar of the immediate.

The widow's loneliness will be heavy since she has been separated from someone she loved. I have been told by women in this situation that the hardest time of the day for them is after sunset. There are several ways to cope with this. One is to plan ahead so that you always have something to look forward to in the immediate future. Perhaps you could get involved in an evening Bible study, enroll in adult night school, take a creative art course, or even learn a new hobby. Some of the best hospital volunteer workers are widows. Whatever you do, it is necessary to take your eyes off yourself and recognize that God is your refuge and a very present help in trouble.

It is not a sin to be lonely, nor is it a sign of weakness. God created us with a need for other people. He also created us in His image, and we have a need for His fellowship. It is right to seek both the fellowship of God and the companionship of people. The important factor is to keep them balanced and not forsake one for the other. Prolonged loneliness reveals that we are deficient in either or both of these God-given desires.

There will be many well-meaning couples who will try to include the woman who has been left alone, either through divorce or death, in their social plans. This usually makes her feel even more alone since the others around her have a partner, and she goes home by herself to an empty house. To you married couples who have included single women in your plans, it would be far better to invite two of them so they are not made to feel like the odd person. One woman in this situation told me that she was so frustrated and upset when her friends tried to include her that she began to refuse any invitations to go out. She desired to be socially involved, but an evening with friends left her in such a miserable state, she felt it was not worth it. It was then that she met another widow who was experiencing the same problems. They became friends and began to accept invitations together rather than separately. As they met other women who were alone, they included them in their nights out. These two women were soon the nucleus of a group of women who enjoyed doing many things together. One of them was a good Bible teacher, so they decided to meet once a week for Bible study and fellowship. They became avid hockey fans, and instead of two women going to the games, they usually had a group of eight or ten. The last I heard, these women were planning a trip to Germany in the near future. Whether or not they are able to go, they at least have had the fun of planning and anticipating the trip. They no longer appear to be lonely since they have learned to share their lives with other women who need each other.

For years we were friends with a lovely couple who had two daughters. It was obvious that the man in this home was the tower of strength for his family and led them in establishing a beautiful Christ-centered home. It was a major blow to the wife when her husband was suddenly stricken with a heart attack and, after just a short period of illness, the Lord called him home. This lady had leaned on him so heavily that she did not know how to handle business matters well enough to run a home. There were decisions to make that she had never before been confronted with. Her daughters needed her to lean on for strength and security at this time, and she began to crumble. It seemed as though her whole world was caving in. Her insecurity, fear, and heartache caused her to withdraw from her friends. She needed them now more than ever, but she chose to close them out of her life. Loneliness set in. Her self-image grew less and less. Her God-given desires and need for fellowship were off-balance. In separating herself from human companionship, she was also losing out on her fellowship with God. It was sad to see this beautiful family disintegrating before us. The change did not come about suddenly, but after much prayer and insistence from her friends, they were able to draw her out of herself and restore their fellowship with her. It seemed as though her increased fellowship with people corresponded with her spiritual growth and communion with Christ.

The Lord Jesus promises a more abundant life to *all* who come to Him and allow the Holy Spirit to control their broken and mixed-up lives; that includes the woman without a husband.

> I am come that they might have life and that they might have it more abundantly.
>
> *John 10:10b*

15

EVERY WOMAN CAN SERVE GOD!

"I could never do that!" This is the response given many times by women who genuinely believe they cannot do a specific service for God. Most of the time they are secretly wishing they could.

There is a place of Christian service suited for every woman, regardless of her temperament. Certainly there are some who will never be pianists, some who will never sing solos or even sing in the choir, and some who will never teach a Bible class. But for the most part we are too quick to respond that we cannot do a job without consulting our Heavenly Father to see what He wants us to do.

Each temperament has certain natural weaknesses related to Christian service, but when the Holy Spirit controls our lives, we can say, "I can do all things through Christ who strengtheneth me" (Philippians 4:13). Let Christ decide what the "all things" should be. It is important that each of us has some area of ministry that we might be obedient and spiritually fulfilled. When we take in the rich blessings God has for us through His Word but never share them with others, we become spiritually stagnant. God has promised to provide the ability if we provide the willing spirit and the dedicated heart.

Musical Martha Melancholy

Martha will never volunteer for a place of service unless she is first motivated by the Holy Spirit. However, if she is mixed with the sanguine temperament, she may first volunteer and later regret that she has done so. Her poor self-image and pessimistic nature usually cause her to feel that she is not capable of doing much of anything. Because of this she will probably feel more comfortable working with children rather than her own peer group. They will accept her as she is while her peers may think she is inadequate for the job.

Since the melancholic is generally the artistic, gifted person, she will probably have musical talent but will be reluctant to use it. Her performmance will never be up to her expectations, even after long hours of practice.

It is best not to put her in a position in which she must meet strangers, since this may cause her to withdraw and be unhappy with her work. She lives in a world of her own and thus would not make a good counselor.

On the positive side, she is best suited for keeping records or doing detailed work. This may be anything from taking attendance in a Sunday School department to managing the records for the church treasury. She has a very neat, orderly system and often makes a good bookkeeper. Whatever she attempts to do, she can be counted on for faithfulness and dependability. It is true that Martha does not attempt to do too much. She conserves her energy, but she finishes whatever she undertakes.

When she is a Spirit-controlled woman, she will have the ability to do many of the things that are difficult and foreign to her natural temperament. I have seen Spirit-controlled Melancholy Marthas become so outgoing and self-confident that they are hardly the same person.

Our church has a program designed for welcoming people as they enter the church for services. Each Sunday a different couple is appointed to stand at the front door of the church for about thirty minutes before services begin. They shake hands and greet everyone who enters. I find this a delightful experience because I never know who will be there, and many times it is a couple I do not know too well. This is a ministry that every couple can do together. Because opposites attract each other in marriage, often one partner will be outgoing and the other more retiring. The greeters certainly represent this idea. Usually one of them will grab a hand to shake before the person is all the way in the door, but the other will be more reluctant to do so. One Sunday I was taken by surprise; not one partner but both of them grabbed my hand to shake it and literally pulled me through the door. What a greeting that was, and how unusual to find two partners so outgoing. I later learned that the woman at the door had only recently been filled with the Spirit.

There had been a time when she had refused to stand there and greet people. Her self-image had been so low that she could not imagine anyone wanting to shake her hand. The Holy Spirit can really make a difference! She now has a ministry of welcoming people into the church. And God is not finished with her yet. It will be exciting to see what other ministries He is preparing for her.

Patient Polly Phlegmatic

Polly is another one who will stand on the sidelines unless she is pressed into service. She is usually satisfied to be a spectator rather than a participant. Once she is motivated and challenged, you can expect her to do an excellent job. Her dependable and consistent nature makes her a delight to work with.

Since she is a gentle, patient person who is easy to get along with, she is well suited for work with children. Children can sense her genuinely kind spirit and respond very readily to her. She has the potential for being a good teacher.

It is best not to give her work that must be done in a hurry. She does excellent work but is known to be rather slow, because she works very carefully and thoroughly. She performs well under pressure; however, she does not like to be put in this situation.

By nature she does not get too involved with other people, and this makes her appear indifferent to their needs. Because of her calm spirit and her ability to remain neutral in considering both sides of a problem, she can make a very good counselor.

The same thing is true for Polly as it was for Martha: the Holy Spirit can enable her to do many of the things that seem contrary to her natural temperament. But she must first be willing to be controlled by the Spirit. I have watched the progress of one very phlegmatic woman. At first she was very careful of her involvement and protected herself from outside influences that might cause her to participate. It appeared as though she had an impenetrable protective shell around her. Even her area of service, working with children, limited her: she felt extremely comfortable working with children and could perform this service in her own strength without too much dependence on the Lord. Finally, that protective shell developed a crack and the Holy Spirit was able to get through to her. It was beautiful to watch the transformation that took place in this woman over the next several months. She completely yielded herself to Christ and asked to be filled with the Holy Spirit. She even asked to be used in a new ministry in which she would become totally dependent upon the power of the Spirit for help. This is exactly what happened! Now she is out on a spiritual limb that is being supported by her Heavenly Father. If He should let go, there would be no way she could rescue herself. That is total dependence upon Christ!

Capable Clara Choleric

This lady is very unlike Martha and Polly, who have problems with their self-image. Clara has an overabundance of self-confidence and has a rather great opinion of herself. Because of this she usually will not participate in anything unless she is the leader and in full control. The incompetence of others disgusts her to the point that she would just as soon do the job herself.

Her ability to be a good organizer and a capable promoter results in effective production. Opposition does not slow her down; on the contrary, it is an exciting challenge for her.

The pioneering spirit that she possesses is a real asset for her in beginning and organizing a new work and ministry. Her self-motivation and drive will get her started, and she will see a job through to completion.

Usually she is not interested in being a counselor because she has neither time nor interest in the problems of others. She most likely would become very impatient with the weaknesses of those whom she counseled.

It is best not to place her in a department with children. Because of her impatience and explosive hot temper, she will not be able to tolerate the working conditions necessary for doing children's work.

She is well suited to be the leader of a committee or department. Some may interpret her leadership as that of a dictator, but if this is the case, it is because of her desire and drive to reach the goals set before her. In pursuing these goals, she may step or even run over some people. When working with a Clara-type, it is best to move with her or, if you can't keep up, to at least stay out of her way. However, the Holy Spirit can soften and change even this temperament trait to make her more congenial and sensitive to those she is working with.

Our Vacation Bible School was directed one summer by a very capable Clara Choleric. She accepted the job rather late in the year when everyone else had turned it down. Realizing that she had to proceed faster than usual because of the loss of time, she plowed into that program with record-breaking speed. I have never seen lesson preparations pulled together so quickly, much less all the detailed work of planning the crafts and ordering the materials. She had the Bible school staffed almost immediately and, believe it or not, by opening day all was ready and in order. That program ran smoothly and efficiently on the surface, but underneath were the battle-scars and wounds of those who had stood in her way as she marched toward that goal. Finally, the wounded rallied and began to drop out one by one. The pastor had to work full-time to patch up the wounds Clara had inflicted and to apply spiritual bandaids in an attempt to restore peace and harmony. He was able to salvage some of the wounded and the Bible School continued. But how much more could have been accomplished if Clara had been controlled by the Holy Spirit. She evidently felt she had to do it all by herself and she nearly failed. God was willing to use her strengths to organize and promote, but she needed His help to be loving and sensitive to the needs of others. Cholerics need to be Spirit-controlled!

Smiling Sarah Sanguine

This cheerful lady is one of the most active in Christian work. She is very quick to volunteer her services in many different areas. Unfortunately, she is not too disciplined and is often late or undependable in what she promises to do.

Children love Sarah because she is a great story-teller. She can dramatize and embellish stories so that they come to life for boys and girls. Since she is uninhibited, she can easily let herself go and participate in their games and stunts. She enjoys having children look up to her because it seems to satisfy a need she has—that of being in the limelight.

The church visitation program will be enhanced by Sarah's participation. She meets people well and is extremely cordial and enthusiastic. Her charisma draws many to her; thus, she always has many friends.

It is difficult for her to be in full charge of a program because she is disorganized and usually unproductive. She has been known to commit rather serious blunders, but because most people love her, they are willing to overlook many of these.

Her counseling is not too sound, since she is very quick to give advice without considering all sides to a story. Interestingly enough, she has many who want to share their problems with her because of her winsome ways. Also, the fact that she generally takes sides with the party she is listening to causes some to be drawn to her.

The Holy Spirit has so much to offer Sarah in the way of self-discipline. She already is a willing worker. Her need is to be a dependable willing worker! We have all seen very capable people lose their effectiveness because they could not be dependable. One such lady—a charming, lovable sanguine—volunteered to direct the Junior Choir in our church. The children loved her, and the choir grew instantly in number. It seemed that all was going well until one day a parent decided to sit in on the choir practice while she waited for her child. Practice was scheduled to start at four o'clock. At 4:10 the director had not arrived. There were thirty-five active junior boys and girls assembled. I wish I could say they were sitting with their hands folded, waiting patiently for the director to arrive. But that would not be true nor would it be normal. Instead, there were boys chasing girls, boys throwing books at boys, and girls hopping from chair to chair. Finally, at 4:20 the choir director came rushing in, panting for breath and smiling apologetically as she grabbed the boys and girls and pulled them into their chairs. She hurriedly explained to the concerned parent that she had been shopping and time had slipped by before she realized she was late. The children later told the parent that this happened every week; they always had to wait for her. The final straw came when the Junior Choir was scheduled to sing in church one Sunday evening. The children arrived and sat in the pews designated for the choir. Church was to start at seven, and the children were all in their places by that time. They looked darling! The boys had their shirttails tucked in and their hair neatly combed; the girls wore ruffled dresses and had their hair curled to perfection. The parents were obviously excited and thrilled as they marched their starry-eyed youngsters down to the front and placed them in the proper pew. The service started and Sarah still had not arrived. By 7:30 it seemed apparent that she was not coming, so the pastor asked the choir to stand and sing without their director. Their self-confidence had been somewhat shaken by this time, and although they performed, everyone was certain they had not done their best. There were thirty-five boys and girls who felt that the director had let them down. And rightly so! Would you believe that Sarah had gone out of town and forgotten this momentous occasion! At the next choir practice ten boys and girls were present. Sarah's effectiveness as a choir director was gone. She had disappointed the children and probably angered the parents. Oh, how she needed the help of the Holy Spirit in her life to make her more disciplined and dependable.

Every woman can serve God! We can say with Paul,

> Whereof I was made a minister [or a teacher, a choir director, or whatever God calls us to do] according to the gift of the grace of God given unto me by the effectual working of his power. Unto me who am less than the lest of all saints [any temperament], is this grace given, that I should preach among the Gentiles the unsearchable riches of Christ.
>
> *Ephesians 3:7-8*

He can use anyone who has a willing heart, a dedicated life, and a prayer to be filled with the Holy Spirit.

There is a need, however, for the Christian woman to keep a proper balance of activities in her life. It is possible that she can get so involved in her service for the Lord that she neglects those things, such as her family and home, that should have top priority. If a mother is so busy that she cannot pay proper attention to her husband or listen attentively to her children, she will not be able to do an effective work for the Lord. On the other hand, some women use their home and families as an excuse for not getting involved. There must be a proper balance—we must serve our families, our home, and our Heavenly Father.

> Let your moderation be known unto all men. The Lord is at hand.
>
> *Philippians 4:5*

16

THE SECRET OF
THE SPIRIT-CONTROLLED
WOMAN

"Why do I always do the wrong thing?" wept a Christian wife and mother who sought help. It is an old story. She knew what to do when faced with certain temptations, but she succumbed to their lures anyway. Naturally, they usually fell in the area of her temperament weaknesses. As is the case with everyone else, her strengths, talents, and abilities were being nullified by her ever-present weaknesses. Only when she learned how to walk in the Spirit was she able to overcome them. It didn't happen overnight, for she had walked in the flesh, obeying her weaknesses, for so long she had deeply ingrained habits. But gradually she learned the art of walking in the

Spirit. It has changed her life!

Success in all the circumstances and stages of life is dependent on walking in the Spirit. Lest I make the same mistake a noted Bible teacher made in our church, we should examine carefully how to walk in the Spirit. One Sunday when this man was the guest speaker, he delivered the morning message on the Spirit-filled life. It was a masterpiece! He had made walking in the Spirit so attractive and appealing that, by the time he finished, he had everyone in the auditorium thirsty to be filled with the Spirit as Paul commands in Ephesians 5:18. My husband was so moved he said to him, "That was fantastic! Tonight I hope you'll tell us how to walk in the Spirit." That dear man of God blinked at my husband and caught his breath. For suddenly he realized that he had neglected the most important part of walking in the Spirit—HOW.

The loving God who commanded "Be ye filled with the Spirit" has provided simple steps to be followed to make this a real possibility:

(1) You must receive salvation by inviting the Lord Jesus into your life. "For whosoever shall call upon the name of the Lord shall be saved" (Romans 10:13). The only means by which you can have your sins forgiven is by calling on the Lord.

(2) You must live in the absolute control of the Holy Spirit. "And be not drunk with wine, in which is excess, but be filled with the Spirit" (Ephesians 5:18). The words "filled" and "controlled" are interchangeable. In each place the Bible speaks of "being filled with the Spirit" it also means "being controlled by the Spirit."

(a) Our minds affect how we behave, so it is important that our minds be controlled by the Spirit. "For they that are after the flesh do mind the things of the flesh; but they that are after the Spirit, the things of the Spirit" (Romans 8:5). To mind the things of the flesh leads to death and separation from God. To mind the things of the Spirit results in life and peace, not only peace with God but peace with ourselves. "As a man thinketh in his heart, so is he" (Proverbs 23:7). What we are governs what we think, how we think governs how we act, and how we act governs our relationship to God. Our thoughts, our actions, and our relationship to God are all affected when we are controlled by the Spirit.

(b) When sin enters our life, the filling of the Holy Spirit is immediately cut off. Therefore, we must regularly confess our sin to Christ. "If we confess our sins, he is faithful and just to forgive us our sins, and to cleanse us from all unrighteousness" (1 John 1:9).

(3) You must read the Word regularly. It is interesting to note the comparison of the results of the Spirit-filled life and the Word-filled life.

Results of Spirit-filled Life (Ephesians 5:18-21)

1. Joyous heart
2. Thankful spirit
3. Submissive attitude

Results of Word-filled Life (Colossians 3:16-18)

1. Joyous heart
2. Thankful spirit
3. Submissive attitude

Obviously, if you are going to walk in the control of the Spirit, you must know the mind of the Spirit. This is not derived by visions or revelations but by studying the Word of God.

Most women who have come to me for counseling were (1) not controlled by the Spirit and (2) not regularly feeding on the Word of God. You need to spend at least five to fifteen minutes daily reading the Word in order to grow and to walk in the Spirit. Just as looking in the mirror each morning is important for good physical grooming, so looking into the mirror of God's Word is important for daily spiritual grooming.

(4) You must develop a daily sensitivity to grieving the Holy Spirit in your attitudes. This will probably follow a temperament pattern. The phlegmatic and the melancholic tend to sin against the Spirit by worry, anxiety, and fear. The sanguine and choleric grieve the Spirit more through expressions of anger, bitterness, and hostility. "Grieve not the Holy Spirit of God by whom ye are sealed unto the day of redemption" (Ephesians 4:30).

A dedicated Christian lady once confessed to me that she was deteriorating rapidly in her Christian life. I had always thought of her as extremely outgoing, attractive, and gracious in spirit. She had been the instrument God had used to lead first her husband and then her three teen-age children to Christ. But through her tears she told quite a different story: "For the past few months my nerves have been on edge. I snap at my husband, yell at my children, and the other day I got so mad I stamped my foot and swore. That's the way I used to act before I became a Christian."

To my question, "What is the most traumatic experience you have had during the past few months?" she hesitantly answered, "Learning that my husband has had an affair." Her melancholic husband had become so exercised in his conscience after his conversion that he felt compelled to admit his infidelity to his wife.

Interestingly enough, she had forgiven her husband, realizing that his sin was cleansed by the blood of Christ, and she had accepted his promise that he would never see the woman again; her husband was not the difficulty. The problem was that she knew the woman! In fact, the woman was an old family friend and a professing Christian with whom she had once prayed for her husband's salvation. Now every time she thought of that woman, she would get angry. "The very idea of her betraying my trust and friendship really irritates me," she said. As she made that statement, I noticed she grew tense and her hand began to tremble. Calling her attention to her trembling hand, I commented, "That woman really gets to you, doesn't she?" And at that she exploded with fury and ended up sobbing.

By this time it was even obvious to her that bitterness and hate were consuming her and that she had to do something about it. We examined a few verses on forgiveness (Matthew 6:14, for example), and she was ready to confess her hatred for this woman to God. Gradually she began to "forget those things that are behind" and started walking in the Spirit. Today she is once again that radiant Christian of former days because she no longer grieves the Holy Spirit with the attitude of her heart.

If you can "walk in the Spirit" in your mental and spiritual attitudes, you will walk in the Spirit in your actions. That is why walking in the Spirit is based on the personal relationship we maintain with God. For truly our relationship to Him is the key to how we get along with everyone else.